A gift for:

_____

From:

_____

Date:

_____

Blessings for Mothers:
Stories, Verse, and Insights to Celebrate the Joy of Motherhood

ISBN: 0-8307-4199-2
Copyright © 2005 Mark Gilroy Communications, Inc.
All rights reserved.

Printed in the U.S.A.

Design by Greg Jackson, Thinkpen Design LLC, Springdale, AR

Any omission of credits is unintentional.
The publisher requests documentation for future printings.

BLESSINGS FOR MOTHERS

STORIES, VERSE, & INSIGHTS TO CELEBRATE THE JOY OF MOTHERHOOD

Regal

From Gospel Light
Ventura, California, U.S.A.

Contents

Making the decision to have
a child is momentous.
It is to decide forever to have
your heart go walking around
outside your body.

ELIZABETH STONE

Becoming a Mommy

There's nothing quite like finding out you're about to become a mom. It's a completely unique mix of ecstatic joy, fear, unspeakable love, and gratitude. And it only gets better as our first child grows and we add on to our family—our hearts somehow stretch to love our kids even more deeply than we ever thought possible. One thing's for sure: Our lives are never the same again.

Children are a gift from the LORD;
they are a reward from him.

PSALM 127:3

Suddenly she was here.
And I was no longer pregnant;
I was a mother. I never
believed in miracles before.

ELLEN GREENE

The Gift of Motherhood

STEPHANIE WELCHER THOMPSON

I spend a lot of time in a rocking chair, coaxing five-month-old Micah to sleep. Sometimes she gets so tired that she cries and screams before she finally nods off out of sheer exhaustion. Not I. Being a mother has taught me to snooze whenever and wherever I can. Once while we were rocking, I woke Micah when my chin hit the top of her head. I'd rocked myself to sleep.

Napping in an upright position isn't the only thing my daughter has taught me. Before my mothering career, my uniform consisted of tailored suits, high heels, hose, and a briefcase. I prided myself on accessories, choosing coordinating earrings, necklaces, and bracelets for each outfit.

Micah was six weeks old when I resumed my duties hosting a weekly radio show. One afternoon, I dressed professionally to see a client. As I picked up Micah to say goodbye, she spit up on my collar. When I pulled her away from my neck, a tiny hand reached out and grabbed the necklace I'd carefully chosen. Unloosening her grip, I accidentally poked her in the head with an earring.

Successful dressing now requires wash-and-wear shirts instead of jackets that need to be dry cleaned. Chains that can be pulled or earrings that scratch are left in the jewelry box. Spit-up is an everyday occurrence, but I consider it my badge of honor.

Besides rearranging my clothing priorities, having a baby has taught me the true meaning of accomplishment. After twenty-two years in journalism, I've won several awards. But the trophies and plaques adorning the wall in my home office pale in comparison to my latest achievement with my daughter.

The nasal aspirator had remained a mystery to me ever since I brought Micah home from the hospital—I've always been able to delegate that task to my mother, since she plays with Micah each afternoon while I work. One evening, Micah had an excessive amount of fluid in her nose, leaving me no choice: in order for her to breathe, I had to learn to work the bulbous device to eradicate the build-up. It took about twenty minutes of concentrated effort on both our parts, but I finally achieved success.

About that time, my husband, Michael, came home.

"Honey," I hollered. "You've got to see this."

Michael walked into the nursery.

"Look at all this snot I got out of the baby's nose," I said with pride as I displayed a thoroughly wet tissue.

Needless to say, Michael did not share my elation.

At that moment, I realized that I had officially moved from being a woman with a baby to being a mother.

Yes, now I split my time between a desk chair and a rocking chair, but the hours I spend in the nursery are changing my life. While praying for Micah to fall asleep each day, I often thank God for giving us a precious daughter and blessing me with the gift of motherhood. ⬡

From now on all generations
will call me blessed,
for the Mighty One has done
great things for me—
holy is his name.

LUKE 2:48-49

A Great First Impression

NANCY B. GIBBS

"Sandy's having contractions," Brad announced when he called his mom, Sarah Ann. Since they lived three hours apart, Sarah Ann left work immediately, rushing home to pack. She wanted to be there when her newest grandbaby was born.

While waiting for her husband to get home from work, Sarah Ann called her son to see how close together the contractions were. A friend of the family answered.

"May I speak to Brad or Sandy?" she asked.

"They're not here."

"Oh, my!" Sarah Ann exclaimed. "They must be at the hospital already."

"No," the voice said, "Brad's getting lunch and Sandy's getting her nails done."

Confused, Sarah Ann wondered, "I thought Sandy was in labor."

"She is," the friend said. "But she said she wanted to have perfect fingernails when she welcomed her baby into the world." ⬡

God makes the world
all over again,
whenever a little
child is born.

JEAN PAUL RICHTER

The first handshake in life
is the greatest of all:
the clasp of an infant fist
around a parent's finger.

MARK BELTAIRE

Love, Mom

Do you remember how you felt when you first found out you were pregnant? When you first felt the baby kick?

If pregnancy is in your near future, keep a running letter to your unborn child—let them know what's on your mind and heart as you wait for their arrival. This would make a great thirteenth birthday gift!

For your older kids, write a similar letter letting them know how much you looked forward to meeting them for the first time, how much you enjoy spending time with them, and how much they mean to you.

Surprise is the greatest gift
which life can grant us.

BORIS PASTERNAK

A Baby for You

PATRICIA DAVIS

When Dawn walked through my front door that Sunday in January, she was six months pregnant with her first child. "Surprise!" we all shouted.

How could I say no when Dawn's mother asked if she could have the shower here? We spent that morning decorating the living room, dining room, kitchen, and breakfast room with streamers and balloons of blue and pink. Family and friends of the mother-to-be brought various hot and cold dishes, a few rich desserts, and several sweetly wrapped gifts for the new arrival. My niece was twenty-two, excited about the forthcoming birth and surprised by the shower.

I was excited too, and had been so ever since I heard those life-altering words back in September: "Jeanne, I have a baby for you." I knew my life would never be the same.

Two years ago, after the latest surgery to remove a cyst on my ovary due to endometriosis, I was left with only a fourth of one ovary, making it unlikely if not impossible that I would ever become pregnant. So my husband, John, and I decided to pursue a private, independent adoption.

I was now forty-six years old and awaiting the birth of the baby who would be my son. I had none of the physical discomfort of carrying him, but felt all the joy and anticipation my niece was experiencing. Neither John nor I had a clue about caring for a newborn, but somehow I was sure we would be perfect parents— we certainly couldn't be happier or more eager parents-to-be.

Almost no one at the shower that day knew I was about to leave my job, ready our home for a child, decorate a room as a nursery, and buy clothes for an infant. I wanted so much to shout to everyone I knew that we would soon be parents. But that would have to wait—the birth was a month away, and I wanted to keep things quiet until the adoption was completely settled. Besides, this was Dawn's day. I was happy for us both.

Johnny was born on a Sunday one month later. Now my good news was out, and his birth announced to everyone in our family. All my friends had long since raised their children—most had children in college, and one was already a grandmother. When they heard about the new little man in my life, they all got together and conspired, and the next baby shower was for my son and me.

Life with my son changed me. Our baby taught us what it felt like to be parents, and introduced us to a love that shocked us both. Still a couple months from delivery, Dawn called me to ask, "What's it like being a mom?"

I clued her in on all my experiences with a newborn. "Well, Johnny cried for hours last night. John rocked him gently and eventually he fell asleep." When she became apprehensive about being a mommy, I reassured her that she most definitely would manage. I think watching me go just before her in becoming a mother gave her confidence that she would be able to handle the challenges.

Her daughter, Stephanie, was born in April. We spent many hours together and over the phone discussing our new infants. We shared our discoveries and which approaches were working or not working for us in caring for our babies.

The following year, on Mother's Day, the family got together for the day at my sister-in-law's home. Dawn was expecting her second child and showing at four months. My son was walking now. The demands of an active child on me, an older mom, had become exhausting. I'd been feeling ill for a several weeks in a row, so I made a doctor's appointment for the next day.

I was stunned when I heard the doctor's diagnosis. "The

pregnancy test is what?" Impossible. I was forty-eight and infertile. After the initial astonishment and joy subsided, I couldn't help but wonder how I would cope with two small children at my age. And would my baby be healthy? I started to worry.

Before long, I was showing, a little soccer ball beginning to bulge in my tummy. This time around, my niece and I wore maternity clothes at the same time. She reassured me everything would be fine. "I know all about being pregnant. Forget your age," she reassured me. I wasn't sure her advice was exactly scientific, but it certainly was encouraging.

And she was right. My initial worry was unnecessary. It was a thrilling time in my life, having one child and another on the way. My pregnancy was pleasantly normal and uneventful, although I did experience the expected morning sickness, tiredness, and a little edema in my ankles.

I had planned on natural childbirth, and John and I attended all the classes for expectant mothers. Even with all our preparation, though, fear arose in my heart again as my December due date approached. And then the day finally came when I went into labor. After several somewhat rocky hours and a C-section, Joshua was born, full term and healthy at eight pounds, six ounces.

As I entered my life as a mother of two, I wondered if it would feel different to mother my biological son. But the love I felt for both of them was the same. Johnny was our first child, and we experienced all the wonder of having a brand new baby in the house, a wonder that returned in full when Joshua, our surprise blessing, entered our home. Getting to know both of them has been the most wonderful experience of my life. I'm mommy to them both.

Dawn's two girls and my two boys are close in age, and they all go to school together. And she and I are not just relatives but friends and comrades in childbearing and parenting. I don't think anyone could have written a more unique story than ours; but I wouldn't have it any other way. ⬡

He settles the barren woman in her home
as a happy mother of children.

PSALM 113:9

Dear Heavenly Father,

Every time I look at my child, I'm amazed and humbled and grateful to have someone to love this much.

Thank You for blessing me with children. Thank You for that moment when I first found out I was about to be a mother. Thank You for the way my children have changed my life—the way they've changed me.

Lord, You know how much I want to be a good steward of this gift You've given me. I pray that You would give me strength and grace to be the best mom I can be. And renew my gratitude, Lord—remind me every day that my children are precious gifts.

Thank You for the joy You've given me.

The best things in life aren't things.

ART BUCHWALD

Everyday Joys

Life is wonderful with kids in the nest—hectic, yes,
but wonderful. It's especially wonderful when we open
our eyes of gratitude and see the joy in little things.
Nothing can quite compare to having your son ask you to
marry him when he grows up, or having your daughter
hand you a fistful of dandelions. The greatest mothering
joys are the smallest.

How wonderful it is, how pleasant,
when brothers live together in harmony!

PSALM 133:1

*Being a full-time mother is one
of the highest salaried jobs in my field,
since the payment is pure love.*

MILDRED B. VERMONT

Right Where I Want to Be

WENDY DUNHAM

Forget movies and fine dining on a Saturday night—I was having fun at home. My daughter, Erin, had just transformed our bathroom into a beauty parlor and could hardly wait to begin my makeover.

I watched Erin as she strategically and deliberately arranged her play makeup and Barbie cologne on our vanity. She had chosen deep orchid lipstick (purple), peony nail polish (neon pink), lavender eye shadow (with sparkles, of course), and bright pink blush (the name "bubble-gum flash" might have been more accurate).

As she lavishly applied the purple lipstick to my lips, Erin stepped back and said, "Mom, you look so great!" Then with all her six-year-old sincerity, she looked at me as if I were the most beautiful woman in the world. And for those few moments, I believed I was.

With her tiny doll comb, she "fixed" my hair so it was flat against my head, and then she looped her plastic pearls around my neck. "Wait here, Mom," she said, "I'll be right back," and soon returned with earrings. "I've picked just the right ones," she declared and held out her palm to display my jingle-bell earrings. Being six, she didn't care that Christmas was four months ago.

Next she brought in my wedding shoes. As she slipped them on my feet, I was Cinderella at last. It wasn't long, however, before my feet were numb and my toes tingled—ankle socks and fallen arches left little room for comfort. But I kept them on, for we hadn't yet had our dance.

For the finishing touch, Erin tied two scarves together for a shawl and placed them over my shoulders. "There, Mom," she said. "You're gorgeous!"

When we finally danced our dance, that night I was the most beautiful (and the most blessed) mother in the whole world. My grown-up soul had been restored with the joy, hope, and wonder of a child. And as we waltzed through our living room, I couldn't help but think, *This is right where I want to be.*

Sometimes being a mom can get pretty overwhelming. But something I've found to be helpful is to keep a journal to remind myself of all the times when being a mom is the greatest life anyone could have. This Saturday night with my daughter was a perfect journal entry. Along with the night all four of us camped in the backyard and the afternoon we brought home our new puppy, it's sure to recharge my mommy batteries and fill my joy cup for years to come. ⬡

He gives children to the woman
who has none and makes her a happy mother.

PSALM 113:9

Wildflowers

NANCY B. GIBBS

The young mother sat staring out the window. She had spent most of the day alone and missed her daughter. She couldn't wait for the school bell to ring. Suddenly, she saw her daughter, Becky, running across the field toward home.

The mom jumped up and ran to the door to welcome her. She opened the door to see Becky standing on the front steps with a smile on her face and a fistful of wildflowers in her hands. "These are for you, Mama!" she shouted.

After she hugged Becky and swung her in a circle in the air, the mom pulled out a glass, filled it with water, and placed the tiny bouquet in the middle of the dining room table.

Some people may have seen the floral arrangement as nothing more than a bundle of weeds, but her mother saw them as a perfect centerpiece, a gift from a child's heart. ⬡

The love of a child
is a love like no other.

CRYSTAL QUINN

Any mother could perform
the jobs of several air traffic
controllers with ease.

LISA ALTHER

Rushin' Roulette

CINDY L. HEFLIN

I slapped the snooze bar and rolled over for a few more moments of sleep. *But it's Saturday,* my body pleaded as a beam of sunlight pierced the darkened room and poked me in the eye. Heaving a sigh, I threw off the covers and crawled out of bed.

Still slightly comatose, I stumbled past my husband's unpacked luggage and into the shower. While the steamy spray pummeled my scalp, the day's busy schedule swirled inside my head. I knew I was in severe need of divine assistance, so I quickly shot several arrow prayers heavenward, promising to get to my quiet time a little later.

I pulled on a pair of sweats, dashed downstairs to the kitchen, and pushed a bowl of cereal toward each kid. While they sat crunching at the island, my husband, Bryant, and I checked our mile-long to-do list. As much as we had to do, after a hectic week of school, sports, and business travel, we knew we had to carve out a little family time.

"How about a picnic in the park for lunch?" I suggested. My

gang was game, but a severe storm in the forecast dampened our outdoor plans. Playing it safe, we opted to catch the newest kid-flick at a nearby cinema.

"What if I cook, clean up the house, and finish the party preparations," I offered, "while you shuttle the girls to softball and dance class and take the dog to the vet. Then we could run errands together, and squeeze in the movie before Grandma's birthday bash."

"Okay, girls, let's go!" Bryant called later as the kids scrambled out the door to our sky-blue Caravan. While he taxied our cherubs all over town, I tackled the chores at home. Fun and frantic—just an ordinary Saturday.

The morning evaporated quickly as I wrapped gifts, layered a lasagna, and mopped a trail of muddy paw prints off the kitchen floor. Time continued to slip by as I hurried to rid the countertops of clutter—dirty dishes, star-spangled school papers, a slimy science fair project, and a myriad of books. Feeling a twinge of guilt, I thumbed the pages of my daily devotional and placed it on the table with a pile of mail. "Oh, Father," I whispered. "I'll spend time with You, as soon as I'm finished." My heart longed for a peaceful moment of His presence, but the clock was ticking.

After crossing each item off my checklist, I made a beeline for the bedroom to change clothes and pop in my contacts. Soon, the honking horn in my driveway jolted my mind—I was out of time. I scurried from room-to-room like a squirrel gathering nuts before winter, collecting library books, the dry-cleaning, and an overdue DVD. Checking our bedside clock, I glanced at my Bible with a sigh and hustled out to the van, juggling the load in my arms.

"Just three little errands before the movie, remember?" I panted and dumped the heap into my lap.

"Aw, Mom!" cried the backseat chorus. My husband cruised through the cul-de-sac as the rushin' roulette continued.

Through the afternoon drizzle, we raced the clock, rushing to finish our rounds before show time. Bryant had just returned after another week of business travel, so we made use of our time between stops, bringing Dad up to speed on family concerns and school activities.

"So, what'd you learn about this week?" he asked each child.

"Stranger-Danger!" said our six-year-old with confidence.

Bryant shot a questioning look my way.

"Safety Week at school," I explained with a smile. "The first graders read a booklet and learned rules about crossing the street, riding the bus, and avoiding strangers."

The windshield wipers slurped as we cruised the rain-slick streets and continued our "family time." Halfway through dismantling an involved family issue, we arrived at the crowded superstore to return the overdue DVD. Thunder crashed as Bryant parked at the curb by the door and I rushed in with the video. Just then, lightning crackled and a downpour broke loose. To allow the vehicle behind him access to the entrance, my ever-courteous husband moved ahead a few car lengths. Then the other driver pulled up and parked his sky-blue Caravan at the curb by the door.

Meanwhile, I proceeded through the busy store, straight to the video counter, paid the fee, and headed back. With the grace and speed of a gazelle, I swept by the bargain aisle, squelching my proclivity to browse, and maneuvered my way through the maze of shoppers in the checkout line. I could almost taste the popcorn awaiting us at the theater as I exited the store in sixty seconds—or so.

Reaching the van, I flung open the door, dropped into my seat, and continued our discussion, never skipping a beat. But why wasn't Bryant driving on to the movie? Then I noticed something odd rolling around at my feet. Puzzled, I picked up a fuzzy, fluorescent green tennis ball. "Where'd this come from?" I asked. Confusion furrowed my brow as I casually tossed the ball over the backseat—and turned to my husband for his reply. Sheer terror overwhelmed me when I saw the strange man seated behind the wheel of the van.

Concluding that Bryant and the girls were missing, my mind wildly raced through all the horrible possibilities. I didn't know which to do first: pray or scream. A dead silence hung in the air. Totally numb, I froze with fear like a deer caught in headlights. Come to think of it, the driver looked pretty shocked, too.

Staring out the windshield, I saw another blue mini-van parked straight ahead. Without a word, I bolted out the door and dashed through the rain down the sidewalk. Relief and embarrassment washed over me as I realized my family was right where I'd left them—inside our blue minivan.

They were safe—and completely oblivious to my blunder. While catching my breath, my heart still pounding, I described in detail what had just happened. Bryant listened, an astonished expression on his face, and then suddenly we exploded with laughter. We laughed until our sides ached, tears rolling down our cheeks, and wondered if that poor man was amused too, or just plain shocked.

"Mommy!" my first grader cried over the din. With fear in her voice and tears in her eyes, she was visibly shaken. "Don't you remember? It's not safe to get into a stranger's car!"

After consoling our daughter and assuring her that I wouldn't be making a habit of getting into strangers' cars any time soon, we thanked God for His divine protection before racing to the show.

My nerves calmed as I collapsed into a seat in the darkened theater. Since I'd already experienced the action and adventure of a four-star movie, God finally had my undivided attention. *Be still, My child, and know that I am God,* I sensed Him whisper, as my heart overflowed with the peace of His presence. I sighed, grateful for peaceful moments—and moments of laughter—that punctuated the rushin' roulette and gave me strength. ⬡

You will fill me with joy in your presence,
with eternal pleasures in your right hand.

PSALM 16:11

A Walk in the Woods

To make today a special day in your children's memories, plan a walk in the woods. You obviously need to consider the ages of your children when determining the kind of terrain you will explore and the distance of your walk. But get as far away from the ordinary as you can on a day trip.

If your children are younger, provide them with a bag to "collect" things that interest them. They'll love this part of your activity even if all they pick up are twigs and rocks. For older children and teens (and yourself), supply a journal. Toward the end of the day, set aside time to write down impressions of God's creation and your time together as a family—and then write a prayer of thanksgiving for the wonderful world and beautiful today He has made.

The family. We were a strange little band
of characters trudging through life
sharing diseases and toothpaste,
coveting one another's desserts,
hiding shampoo, borrowing money,
locking each other out of our rooms,
inflicting pain and kissing to heal it
in the same instant, loving, laughing,
defending, and trying to figure out the
common thread that bound us all together.

ERMA BOMBECK

*Above all, love each other deeply,
because love covers over
a multitude of sins.*

1 PETER 4:8

Dear Heavenly Father,

There are thousands of little things that make being a mom such a wonderful joy. I pray, Lord, that You would open my eyes to see those little wonders throughout the day. Help me see Your grace in my child's smile, in a settled argument. Lord, may my decisions and interactions with my kids be filled with Your grace as well.

Father, thank You—thank You for these precious kids.

A mother's love for her child
is like nothing else in the
world. It knows no law, no pity,
it dares all things and crushes down
remorselessly all that stands in its path.

AGATHA CHRISTIE

A Mother's Love

Our love for our kids started before they were born and deepened with each passing day. We delighted when they learned to turn over; we rushed to their side every time they cried. And our lives are enriched when we realize that God loves us the same way—patiently, attentively, passionately. A mother's tender love—much like our Father's—has softened and soothed many a hard, broken heart.

As a mother comforts her child,
so will I comfort you.

ISAIAH 66:13

If you have never been hated
by your child you have
never been a parent.

BETTE DAVIS

Tough Love

JANICE ALONSO

As a mom, I always found it easy to be loving. I found it harder to be tough.

It got even harder when my two sons hit their teenage years. Loving a teen means occasionally having to tell them something they don't want to hear: no. I'm embarrassed to admit that there were times when just being in the same room with my teen boys made my stomach knot. It's not that they were bad kids—I loved them more than life itself. It was just that the little day-to-day confrontations wore me down—this party Saturday night, that outfit, those friends. My husband traveled from Monday to Friday, leaving me to stand alone against the two boys. Some days I felt like I was riding a bucking bronco.

Curfew was the biggest issue in our household and a regular source of standoffs. My curfew rules came in two parts: I wanted to know where each child was going, and when he would return home. Even during their senior year in high school, I set restrictions.

Their parade of complaints never ended. The designated time was too early. Why couldn't they go to parties without adult supervision? No one else had all these stupid rules. They weren't having any fun.

Of course, I wasn't having the time of my life either. The way they looked at me, you would have thought I was the lion tamer in a circus, wielding a whip in one hand and a chair in the other, beating down any chance of freedom these two cubs dreamed of.

Even though I was strict, I didn't think I was unreasonable. I made exceptions when I thought it was fitting—special dances, ballgames played at faraway locations, birthdays. Much to my boys' disbelief, I explained how I'd been a teenager once and knew what it was like to want to have a good time. At one point, in what I suppose was a last-ditch effort to convince them that I was once cool, I dug up my high school yearbook and made my kids read all the nice things my peers had written about me.

"See?" I said. "This one says I'm sweet and a real trip to be around."

Eyes rolled and knowing glances passed between them.

As much as I made efforts to be a lovingly tough mom, I still made mistakes, being a little too soft sometimes, coming down a little too hard other times. Every night and continually throughout the day, I prayed for God's guidance and for requests that would allow more "yeses" so that my kids would see that I wanted them to be happy.

We survived the teen years. My sons are young men now, the older one married but not yet a father. Always the more vocal and resistant regarding our house rules, when he was in law school he gave me a Mother's Day card I'll always treasure. Underneath the printed verse inside, he simply wrote, "Thank you for having the strength to say no when yes would have been so much easier."

I guess being loving and being tough aren't so different after all—sometimes love means saying no. And I know I'm more than blessed to have two sons who recognize my "no's" for what they were: tough love. ⬡

Love never gives up, never loses faith
is always hopeful, and endures
through every circumstance.

1 CORINTHIANS 13:7 NLT

A mother's arms are made
of tenderness and children
sleep soundly in them.

VICTOR HUGO

*Your love has given me
great joy and encouragement.*

PHILEMON 7

A Fighting Chance

CHRISTY PHILLIPPE

Once a week, several young adults from a local church pick up kids from the inner city and bring them to a small group Bible study. One of the questions that Steve, a children's minister at that church, asks the kids is this: "Does your mama love you?" They always answer with an emphatic yes.

Then he asks them why, and they tell him, "She has to—she's my mama!"

Steve has learned one incredible life lesson through the exercise: "Some of the kids sadly might not be able to say if their daddy loves them, because some of them have never met their daddy. But so far, every one of them has said that they know their mama loves them. And that gives all of them a fighting chance to succeed in life."

A mother's love is one of the most powerful life-changing forces in the world today. ⬢

You never get over being a child,
as long as you have a mother to go to.

SARAH ORNE JEWETT

All I am, I owe to my mother.

GEORGE WASHINGTON

My Mother's Care

GLENN A. HASCALL

Most of the children have long since forgotten her, and many have not outlived her, yet for thirteen years my mom was "Mamma" to nearly twenty foster children. Each one unique and amazingly happy. Each one with a desperate need for compassion.

My parents specialized in a specific type of foster care, inviting children to our home who were called "retarded" or "Mongoloid" during that era. Some were autistic (a term we didn't know then), and others couldn't speak.

Many of these kids lived in outlying areas where it was difficult to find educational classes for their special-needs children. Their parents would bring them to our home on Sunday night, and we would care for them through the week, making sure that they got to their special classes at school, that they were fed and bathed, and that all their other needs were taken care of. On Friday afternoon, most of the families would come and pick up their children for the weekend.

Lester didn't talk, but he had a tremendous capacity for joy—if a sound struck him funny, he'd laugh until he cried. Joanie was perpetually curious with a tender heart. Jackie wasn't her sister, but was in

many ways a twin. Rosie was wonderful unless she got mad. Cyndi
never spoke and had fears we could never understand. And there
were others, too many to name.

The only boy who spent a great deal of time with us was John.
He loved music, and he loved to sing. Once, when he was taking a
bath, he thought he was Tarzan and somehow climbed up on the
towel racks. A couple of jumps later, he crashed into the bathtub with
two towel racks and a bit of the wall—didn't seem to faze him a bit.
Mom cleaned him up and sent him on to bed where he'd start sharing
his musical talent with me until the wee hours of the morning.

Mom never seemed to lose her cool with these wonderful kids—not
even the time John decided to dance on top of the chest of drawers with
a record player. One of the legs snapped under the strain of a dancing
little boy, and down came John, the bureau pinning him to the ground
and the record player landing solidly on his chest. When Mom came to
find out what happened, John was not concerned about the piece of
furniture crushing him so much as the record player, still spinning. The
problem was quickly solved and John went back to singing.

Most moms had their hands full with their own children without
adding more youngsters to the mix, especially ones with such specific
and unique needs, but caring for those who needed a little extra care

was Mom's specialty. These children became every bit a part of our family as my sisters and I were, and for years Mom received Mother's Day and Christmas cards from more than a dozen children who thought of her as their second mom.

It's been more than twenty-five years since I last saw any of these "siblings," yet I remember them so clearly—and so fondly. I also remember a mom whose heart was big enough to embrace those that society had little use for. This was a pattern that she demonstrated over and over again throughout her life.

Now in a nursing home, this legally blind woman shares kind words with someone who has had cerebral palsy since she was very young. Mom takes the time to listen and understand what her new friend is saying. She shares a room with a woman who speaks another language, and yet she has found ways to communicate profoundly with someone who is lucid only on rare occasion.

I think God must be pleased. ⬡

I tell you the truth, whatever you did for the least of these brothers of mine, you did for me.

MATTHEW 25:40

The home should be a warm sanctuary
from the storms of life for each member
of the family. A haven of love
and acceptance. Not only children,
but also parents, need this security.

ANONYMOUS

A Little TLC

What did you appreciate most about your mother's love? Was it her kindness and patience? The way she made you feel that no matter what, things would turn out okay? How can you shelter your kids with motherly love today? Right now might be a great time to give your kids an extra hug and an "I love you." And rest assured that your love makes their lives wonderful.

Dear Heavenly Father,

I never knew I could love anyone this much. Lord, thank You so much for my children. Thank You for the special calling to fill their hearts with Your love. I pray that You would give me wisdom and grace to show them what Your love is like—please help me discipline them lovingly and shower them with the kind of tender care You've always given me.

Father, sometimes my love for my kids makes me worry about them. I pray that You would guard my heart with Your peace, and that You would protect my children throughout the day.

And most of all, God, please use me to guide my children to know You.

A child can ask questions
that a wise man cannot answer.

AUTHOR UNKNOWN

A Child's Laughter

One of the best things about being a mom is being around kids. We tend to think of ourselves as the teachers, but some days we end up learning more from them than they learn from us—and they always make sure we have fun doing it.

And he took the children in his arms,
put his hands on them and blessed them.

MARK 10:16

Words of wisdom are spoken
by children at least as often as scientists.

JAMES NEWMAN

Wise in Love

SHERI PLUCKER

The nurse fiddled with something on the other side of the room as I clenched my fists and closed my eyes in prayer.

The doctor entered and introduced himself. "Take a deep breath and relax. This shouldn't take long," he said and reached for the needle. I lifted my head for a quick peek at my massive abdomen as a long, hollow needle penetrated my skin.

"We're just going to draw some fluid to analyze. It should only take a few minutes," the doctor said.

I turned my head to the side and focused on the ultrasound screen. The needle was inserted close to our unborn child, and lingering risk of the amniocentesis returned to my mind once again. Suddenly, I gasped in disbelief at the image on the screen. Our baby reached its hand towards the long needle, and grabbed onto it. My husband and I smiled in awe at our baby's curiosity—it was like she was trying to reach out to us with tiny bits of wisdom and say, "Don't worry. I can't wait to share my love with you."

As I look back on the past five years of mothering a child with

Down syndrome, I find myself amazed by Hailey's ability to reach out with love to every person she encounters—smiling a "thank you" after the nurse pokes her with a vaccine shot, yelling, "Be careful," to the tight rope walker who teeters above at the circus. She spreads her bits of wisdom about love through her voice, affection, and sincere caring for total strangers.

Recently, a relative died in a terrible car accident. After receiving the news, I explained to Hailey what had happened and sunk into a chair, crying. She climbed into my lap, wrapped her arms around me, and cried with me. Minutes later, she lifted her head, gazed into my eyes, and wiped a tear from my cheek.

She smiled and said, "Don't worry, Mom," as she climbed off my lap and disappeared into the bathroom. I heard her rummaging through the cupboard, and moments later she peered around the corner with a smile. She reached her hand towards me and placed a Band-Aid in the palm of my hand.

"Feel better, Mom?" she asked.

A smile swept my tear-stained face. I hugged her, and for that moment the sorrow lifted. My five-year-old daughter had mended my broken heart with a Band-Aid, unconditional love, and a little creativity.

Daily, I try to mirror Hailey's patience, determination, enthusiasm for life, and wonderful, wise love. She has taught me to reach within myself to become a better mother by sharing my love with the world around me.

I smile when I think back to the beginning, to the day we were first introduced and she reached her hand out to me from within my womb. "Mom, Dad, I can't wait to share my love with you." On a daily basis Hailey reveals her love through her smile, laughter, and affection towards others. Hailey is wise in love, well beyond my years as a mother. ⬡

Never let loyalty and kindness get away from you!
Wear them like a necklace; write them deep within your heart.

PROVERBS 3:3 NLT

A Birthday Celebration to Remember

CHRISTY PHILLIPPE

The single mom had to work on her Fourth of July birthday. And to make matters worse, finances were particularly tight that month, so there wouldn't be much of a celebration.

Her nine-year-old son wanted to make a special birthday meal for his mom, complete with a cake and flowers. But he faced a few obstacles. For one thing, he had no idea how to bake a cake. For another thing, his mother didn't allow him to turn on the stove while she was away.

Doing the best he could, he put a package of hot dogs (his favorite meal) in cold water on the stove, then set a two-day-old powdered sugar doughnut on the dining room table, which proudly held an unlighted candle. (Another problem was that he wasn't allowed to strike matches.) Wild honeysuckle blossoms served as the centerpiece.

The mom couldn't help but smile as her "little man" boisterously sang "Happy Birthday" to her when she walked through the door. She boiled the hot dogs and lit the birthday candle. They sat down together and shared a grand birthday celebration she would never forget. ◉

When you look at your life,
the greatest happinesses
are family happinesses.

JOYCE BROTHERS

Children's talent to endure stems
from their ignorance of alternatives.

MAYA ANGELOU

The Little Red Wagon

PATRICIA LORENZ

To be perfectly honest, the first month was blissful. When Jeanne, age six, Julia, four and Michael, three, and I moved from Missouri to my hometown in northern Illinois the very day of my divorce from their father, I was just happy to find a place where there was no fighting or abuse.

But after the first month, I started missing my old friends and neighbors. I missed our lovely, modern, ranch-style brick home in the suburbs of St. Louis, especially after we'd settled into the ninety-eight-year-old white frame house we'd rented, which was all my post-divorce income could afford.

In St. Louis we'd had all the comforts: a washer, dryer, dishwasher, TV, and a car. Now we had none of these. After the first month in our new home, it seemed that we'd gone from middle-class comfort to poverty-level panic.

The bedrooms upstairs in our ancient house weren't even heated, but somehow the children didn't seem to notice. The linoleum floors, cold on their little feet, simply encouraged them to dress faster in the mornings and to hop into bed more quickly in the evenings.

I complained about the cold as the December wind whistled under every window and door in that old frame house. But they giggled about the "funny air places" and simply snuggled under the heavy quilts Aunt Bernadine brought over the day we moved in.

I was frantic without a TV. What would we do in the evenings without our favorite shows? I felt cheated that the children would miss out on all the Christmas specials. But the children were more optimistic and much more creative than I. They pulled out their games and begged me to play Candyland and Old Maid with them.

We cuddled together on the gray tattered couch the landlord provided and read picture book after picture book from the public library. At their insistence we played records, sang songs, popped popcorn, created magnificent Tinker-Toy towers, and played hide-and-seek in our rambling old house. The children taught me how to have fun without a TV.

One shivering December day, just a week before Christmas, after walking the two miles home from my temporary part-time job at a catalog store, I remembered that the week's laundry had to be done that evening. I was dead tired from lifting and sorting other people's Christmas presents, and somewhat bitter, knowing I could barely afford any gifts for my own children.

As soon as I picked up the children at the baby-sitter's, I piled four large laundry baskets full of dirty clothes into the children's little red wagon, and the four of us headed toward the laundromat three blocks away.

Inside we had to wait for washing machines and then for people to vacate the folding tables. The sorting, washing, drying, and folding took longer than usual.

Jeanne asked, "Did you bring any raisins or crackers, Mommy?"

"No," I snapped. "We'll have supper as soon as we get home."

Michael's nose was pressed against the steamy glass window. "Look Mommy! It's snowing! Big flakes!"

Julia added, "The street's all wet. It's snowing in the air but not on the ground!"

Their excitement only upset me more. If the cold wasn't bad enough, now we had snow and slush to contend with. I hadn't even unpacked the box with their boots and mittens yet.

At last the clean, folded laundry was stacked into the laundry baskets and placed two-baskets deep in the little red wagon. It was pitch dark outside. Six-thirty already? No wonder they were hungry! We usually ate at five.

The children and I inched our way into the cold winter evening and slipped along the slushy sidewalk. Our procession of three little people, a crabby mother, and four baskets of fresh laundry in an old red wagon moved slowly as the frigid wind bit into our faces. We crossed the busy four-lane street at the crosswalk. When we reached the curb, the front wagon wheels slipped on the ice and tipped the wagon over on its side, spilling all the laundry into a slushy black puddle.

"Oh no!" I wailed. "Grab the baskets, Jeanne! Julia, hold the wagon! Get back up on the sidewalk, Michael!"

I slammed the dirty, wet clothes back into the baskets.

"I hate this!" I screamed. Angry tears spilled out of my eyes.

I hated being poor with no car and no washer or dryer. I hated the weather. I hated being the only parent responsible for three small children. And if you want to know the truth, I hated the whole blasted Christmas season.

When we reached home I unlocked the door, threw my purse across the room and stomped off to my bedroom for a good cry.

I sobbed loud enough for the children to hear. Selfishly, I wanted them to know how miserable I was. Life couldn't get any worse. The laundry was still dirty, we were all hungry and tired, there was no supper started and no outlook for a brighter future.

When the tears finally stopped I sat up and stared at a wooden plaque of Jesus that was hanging on the wall at the foot of my bed. I'd had that plaque since I was a small child and carried it with me to every house I'd ever lived. It showed Jesus with His arms outstretched over the earth. Obviously solving the problems of the world.

I kept looking at his face, expecting a miracle. I looked and waited, and finally said aloud, "God, can't You do something to make my life better?" I desperately wanted an angel on a cloud to come down and rescue me.

But nobody came—except Julia, who peeked into my bedroom and told me in her tiniest four-year-old voice that she had set the table for supper.

I could hear six-year-old Jeanne in the living room sorting the laundry into two piles: "Really dirty, sorta clean, really dirty, sorta clean..."

Three-year-old Michael popped into my room and gave me a picture of the first snow that he had just colored.

And you know what? At that very moment I did see angels
before me—not one, but three. Three little cherubs, eternally
optimistic and once again pulling me from gloom and doom into
the world of "things will be better tomorrow, Mommy."

Christmas that year was magical as we surrounded ourselves
with a very special kind of love, based on the joy of doing simple
things together. One thing's for sure: Parenthood was never again
as frightening or as depressing for me as it was the night the
laundry fell out of the little red wagon. Those three angels have
kept my spirits buoyed and today, thirty years later, they continue
to fill my heart with the presence of God. ⬡

From the lips of children and infants
you have ordained praise.

PSALM 8:2

I once asked one of my smaller children
what he thought a home was and
he replied, "It's a place where
you come in out of the rain."

GIGI GRAHAM TCHIVIDJIAN

Let the little children come to me,
and do not hinder them,
for the kingdom of God
belongs to such as these.

MARK 10:14

It is in the voice
of our children that we
can hear whispers
of ourselves and the
language of innocence.

CHRISTOPHER DE VINCK

Don't give up trying to do
what you really want to do.
Where there's love and inspiration,
you can't go wrong.

Ella Fitzgerald

I Raised an Angel and a Devil

GWENDOLYN MITCHELL DIAZ

I was trudging through a department store with several toddlers in tow when I spotted a fat red plastic bat with a large white Wiffle ball attached. I recognized immediately that this combination could provide hours of backyard pleasure for my children and become the perfect pastime to fill their long summer afternoons. The fact that it was only $2.99 cinched the decision. I bought it.

As soon as I pulled into the driveway, all of my little boys jumped out of the car, grabbed their new paraphernalia, and headed straight for the back yard. Immediately they started staking out the bases, displaying an incredible depth of knowledge about a game I had never even known them to observe. Picnic benches were moved and boundaries were established. The orange tree was foul, the birdbath was fair, and a home run had to sail over the clothesline. And then the games began.

Before long, paths between the bases had carved themselves into the backyard grass. I spent endless hours pitching to eager batters and reminding youngsters which way to run to first base.

One afternoon I found myself flat on my back, staring at the clouds after having been bashed in the head by a hard-hit Wiffle ball. It was our first indication that Matthew might one day be a slugger. And Zach, who had convinced us that he was a "lefty," soon began striking me out with two well-placed fast balls and a funky curve.

Once the boys had mastered all the backyard basics I had to offer, Dad was enlisted for further coaching. Over the next few years he taught each of our sons how to stand in the batter's box, grip a change-up, and take a secondary lead off first base. He spent endless hours hitting fungoes, evaluating curve balls, raking clay, and driving vanloads of high school boys to faraway fields.

No matter how much we gave them, the boys always wanted more baseball. They quickly moved from Wiffle ballgames in the backyard to Saturday T-ball tournaments at the city field with their buddies. They begged us to sign them up for Little League teams and wouldn't think of missing a single practice. They invited classmates over to watch the "Cubbies" on TV and celebrated birthdays with their teammates at Marchant Stadium.

I realized that baseball had become an obsession when we spent an entire three-week family vacation visiting all the major league ballparks within driving distance. After the trip, my boys could tell

you everything about the teams that played on each field and could
even point out the highest-paid hitters and the wiliest pitchers on
each team. I, on the other hand, could only tell you where to get the
best bratwurst (Milwaukee), which team has the best organist
(Chicago White Sox), and where not to use the restrooms (Boston—
none of the toilets would flush the day we visited Fenway).

As they entered their high school years, my sons began
spending early mornings in the weight room and late afternoons
running long distances around the lake. By this point, most of
their buddies, friends, and teammates had dropped out of the
baseball scene. For my boys, it wasn't all fun and games anymore,
and I often wondered when their enthusiasm would flag. There
were many other activities they had to miss and lots of cold meals
waiting for them at home. But they kept insisting on working hard
to improve their strengths and compensate for their athletic
weaknesses. They've each had to overcome injuries, discouragement, uncooperative college schedules, and various coaches'
idiosyncrasies in order to keep playing the game; but the results
have been astonishing.

This summer, a scout from the Tampa Bay Devil Rays showed
up on our front doorstep and signed Matthew to a professional

contract as a power-hitting outfielder. A few days later we received a call from the Anaheim Angels who needed a left-handed pitcher in their bullpen. Who knows how much longer each of them will choose to stay in the game? But what had started out as a $2.99 impulse buy at the department store turned into a life-changing investment.

As parents, we got them started and taught them a little about baseball along the way. But our kids have taught us major lessons about determination, perseverance, and how to enjoy the gifts God gives. They have each invested a lot of time and energy in the sport, but they've also received a lot of compensation for their dedication.

Baseball has taken them across the country and even to Africa, where Zach participated on a summer "Athletes in Action" baseball team. They have had many outstanding experiences, received college scholarships, made new friends, and had countless opportunities to share their faith.

And me? I've had the unique privilege of raising an "Angel" and a "Devil"! ⬡

Patience and encouragement come from God.

ROMANS 15:5 NCV

You Are Special

What is it that makes your child so special? Is it her love for sunny days? Is it his tender heart? Make a list of five things you love about each member of your family. When you're done, say a prayer of thanks for these very special people in your life.

Dear Heavenly Father,

My children amaze me. Even though it's my job to teach them and impart wisdom, there are so many days when I think they understand so much more than I do—more about simplicity, joy, and what really matters. Lord, thank You for my kids. Thank You for the chance to spend time with them.

Lord, I pray that You would bless them today. I pray that You would make their lives rich and full of good things. And I thank You for loving them even more than I do.

Guide me today, Lord God, as I seek to do what's best for my kids.

A mother is never cocky or proud,
because she knows the
school principal may call at any
minute to report that her
child has just driven a motorcycle
through the gymnasium.

MARY KAY BLAKELEY

The Toughest—and Best—Job in the World

No one ever said it would be easy. They just didn't say there would be days we'd wonder how we would make it to bedtime. The good news is that God gives us grace for the ministry of motherhood and strength for every challenge.

And now, may the God of peace, who brought again from the dead our Lord Jesus, equip you with all you need for doing his will.

HEBREWS 13:20-21 NLT

Children are
God's apostles sent forth,
day by day, to preach of love,
and hope and peace.

JAMES RUSSELL LOWELL

The Miraculous Amid the Mundane

TONYA RUIZ

My oldest daughter was six when I gave birth for the fourth and final time. I expected my life to be like one of Walt Disney's fairy tales where I lived happily ever after in some enchanted, pastel-colored land. Instead, it was like living in the movie *Groundhog Day,* where Bill Murray relived the same day over and over again, starting with a clock radio playing "I've Got You, Babe." That was my life, except without Sonny and Cher.

The dishes were endless, the laundry mountain big enough to ski down. My husband tried to help, but he was overwhelmed too. Every day, I would just barely get caught up with homeschooling and the housekeeping—only to start all over again the next morning.

Little Jeremy was permanently attached to me like a baby gorilla. Zachary struggled with potty training and was inclined to put small items up his nose. The girls, at five and six, went from chaos to crisis. One day, it would be raining Froot Loops. The next day, the kitchen floor would be properly lotioned and turned into an ice rink. I couldn't even take a shower if my husband wasn't home for fear they might burn the house down. As my mother frequently said about my children, "They're not bad; it's just that there are so many of them."

Bedtime was always a difficult task. One night, I was particularly worn out from the endless complaints of "There's a monster in my sock drawer," and "I'm thirsty."

Finally, I thought, *they're asleep.*

And then I heard the giggles. Would they ever just go to bed so I could have some peace and quiet?

As I carried the clean laundry down the hall to put it away, Zachary, a book clutched in his little hands, asked, "Mommy, will you read me this bedtime story?" At three, he couldn't possibly have realized how many "important" things I needed to do before I could go to bed myself.

"Just one," I warned him. While I read sleepily and half-heartedly, Zachary kept interrupting. He was my child of a zillion questions.

"What did you say?" I impatiently asked him.

Zachary repeated, "How did He do that?"

I quickly scanned what I had been reading and said, "Well, Jesus made the fish and bread loaves multiply until all the people had been fed." Zachary stood up on the bed, waved his arms, and excitedly replied, "Mom, that was a miracle!"

Talk about an "ah-ha" moment. I had been so consumed with all the daily tasks that I had taken my eyes off the Lord and become overwhelmed with my circumstances. Even though my pastor often taught, "Your children are gifts from God," I was forgetting to open the gifts, spend time with them, and love them.

I had become like Martha from the Bible. I was so busy serving that I was not spending any time at the feet of Jesus, and I wasn't teaching my children to do so, either. I was so consumed with the miracle of getting to the bottom of the laundry pile that I almost missed the opportunity to teach my children about the awesome miracles of God.

As I tucked Zachary into bed that night, I prayed that God would help me make better choices, use my words wisely, and be the mother that my children needed. And like Bill Murray's character at the end of *Groundhog Day,* I woke up to a new day. ⬡

You will seek me and find me when you
seek me with all your heart.

JEREMIAH 29:13

Raising a teenager is
like nailing Jell-O to a tree.

BARBARA JOHNSON

*What is impossible with men
is possible with God.*

LUKE 18:27

In family life, love is the oil
that eases friction,
the cement that binds
closer together, and the
music that brings harmony.

Eva Burrows

Second Blessings

BARBARA MARSHAK

Twenty-seven hours in a car with six kids—sounded a bit more like punishment than a vacation. My husband insisted on taking the whole family to Florida regardless of any scheduling conflicts.

"None of the kids have spring break the week you can take off work," I noted.

"They won't mind missing school."

"There are eight of us," I reminded him unnecessarily, "and we don't have an RV anymore."

"We can rent one," he quickly countered. I knew then and there that I might as well start packing.

When John and I married, we immediately became a family of seven since he had three children from his previous marriage and I had two daughters from mine. Together with Summer, Krissy, and John Ryan, ages nine, seven, and six, and my girls, Karli and Emily, ages ten and seven, we began our marriage with a pledge to maintain a God-centered foundation, believing we'd been given a second chance to create and build a new family unit. Two years later, we were even more thrilled when our son David was born.

Knowing that a good marriage requires hard work and much prayer, it was gratifying to see the five older kids getting along so well and loving their little brother to pieces. John and I were deeply committed to each other, and with God's guiding hands we were somehow managing to work through issues that could otherwise tear apart a blended family. Even so, throughout our ten years together, I found myself silently comparing ourselves to other families—"intact" families—convinced that for all our efforts we didn't quite measure up to the "perfect" families filling up the church pews on Sunday mornings.

The Counterfeiter knew exactly where I was most vulnerable—family meant everything to me—and he had a way of cutting down my view of our family. *God's design for a family does not include divorce,* he'd subtly whisper. *You're a blemish to the family of God.* And I wilted a little, allowing that seed to take hold.

So, being the realist of the family and struggling with doubt about how we were doing as parents, I was a little skeptical about driving from Minneapolis to Florida with five teenagers stuck together in such close quarters. Would this be pushing things too far? We'd taken this trip once before when the kids were much younger, but now the two oldest girls were in college and used to being on their own. Four girls between sixteen and nineteen—were we crazy? Always the optimist, however, John made the arrangements to rent a twenty-nine-foot recreational vehicle that claimed to sleep eight. And off we went.

Our first stop on a chilly April night was a couple hours south of Minneapolis to pick up Summer from her college dorm. Even though it was already after midnight, John was mentally prepared to drive through the night in order to get the most out of our vacation days. A block from the main highway, he decided to make a quick restroom stop. Several of the kids followed John inside the twenty-four-hour supermarket before I decided to dash inside at the last minute.

In the quietness of the nearly empty aisles I met Emily and Krissy coming out as I went in. When I exited the store a few minutes later, the RV was nowhere in sight. I froze, staring at the vacant parking lot, imagining John and the six kids heading to Florida in the blackness of night—without me. How far would he drive before he realized I'd been left behind? Madison? Chicago? Louisville? I had no purse or money. I didn't know the license plate of the rented RV, and I had no way to contact him. Heart pounding, I didn't know what to do.

What a terrible way to start a vacation, I cried to myself, *and we haven't even left Minnesota yet!* On the verge of outright panic, I caught sight of the RV coming back up the street. "Oh, thank You, Lord," I breathed, racing across the lot.

"I didn't even know you went inside," John explained, "until Emily asked why I didn't wait for you."

Lesson learned and heads were counted at each stopping point thereafter.

As we (all) headed south, temperatures climbed, and by the time we reached sunny Florida, the balmy air was a perfect eighty degrees. Tension from the long drive began to melt away, yet I still wondered if we would all agree on what to do each day. Two of the girls were notorious for sleeping in, and they'd been warned to be up early and ready to go each morning—without complaint.

The first two days at a Disney campground flew by without incident. Funny how hanging out with Mickey Mouse can turn teenagers into giddy kids again. From there we headed west to the shores of Fort Myers, where we had a campsite reserved right on the beach. We set up a small tent alongside the RV to add a little more space since the narrow aisle was forever jammed with duffel bags, sandals, snacks, games, or whatever fell out of the compartments above.

Eating meals on the picnic table seemed the best option, and everyone took turns helping clean up. No one seemed to mind the tropical breeze blowing sand in our food; with lawn chairs perched under palm trees and the surf pounding a few feet away, it sure beat Minnesota in April.

When I scolded the girls about not using enough sunscreen, they simply smilingly pointed to my glowing red shoulders. Hard as we tried, it seemed, our pasty white skin grew tender and sore in the golden Florida sun, but no one seemed to care.

I thought for sure a long afternoon rain shower would be an opportunity for grumbling. But the kids happily played board games inside the camper. Later, the older kids played catch with their little brother as parents and teens took walks—it seemed each one of my pre-trip worries was dispelled by smiles and laughter.

When it was time to head home, I began stuffing everything back in the camper, no longer bothering to keep items in their proper places. Despite the tired bodies, cramped conditions, and lack of privacy, there were no arguments on the long drive north. We arrived home safe and sound, our spirits lifted, our complexion a little browner, and our pocketbook a whole lot emptier.

Several months later, I organized the vacation photos, smiling at the images of our happy faces against the Technicolor ocean. Some shots were posed, others relaxed and casual. But in all of them, we were smiling.

Reliving the trip via color pictures, it struck me: Just as John had been so focused on the long drive that he almost left me stranded in the middle of the night, I had let myself focus on our family's label: blended family.

Yes, we were a blended family—and that was okay. The ten days of vacation mirrored the ten years of our marriage. Things didn't always go as planned—those ten uncertain minutes in the convenience store were certainly unplanned—but we made the best of it. We carried on and enjoyed the days before us.

I selected a particularly smiley group photo of the kids and another of my husband and me and slid them into the collage frame in the hall, front and center. Never again would I forget that God had blessed our family in distinct and wonderful ways, that He had created something wonderful in our little family unit. Blended or not, we were a family. ⬡

Behold, I make all things new.

REVELATION 21:5 NKJV

Bringing up a family
should be an adventure,
not an anxious discipline
in which everybody
is graded for performance.

MILTON R. SAPIRSTEIN

God Never Sleeps

NANCY B. GIBBS

A mother and her four-year-old daughter were preparing for bed one night. The child was afraid of the dark, and the mother, on this occasion, felt a little fearful also.

When the light was out, the child caught a glimpse of the moon outside the darkened window. "Mother," she asked, "is the moon God's light?"

"Yes," answered the mother.

The next question was, "Will God put out His light and go to sleep?"

The mother replied, "No, my child, God never goes to sleep."

Then, with the simplicity of a child's faith, she said: "Well, as long as God's light is on, He's awake, and we might as well go to sleep." ⬡

I would rather walk with God
in the dark than go alone in the light.

MARY GARDINER BRAINARD

So many times we say that we can't serve God
because we aren't whatever is needed.
We're not talented enough or smart enough or whatever.
But if you are in covenant with Jesus Christ,
He is responsible for covering your weaknesses,
for being your strength. He will give you
His abilities for your disabilities!

KAY ARTHUR

Lessons from Shela:
A Daughter's Legacy

LETTIE KIRKPATRICK BURRESS

"Your daughter has a terminal muscle disease. She has only six months to a year to live." This pronouncement came from our pediatrician on Shela's first birthday. But his prediction was wrong by about eighteen years.

No other single circumstance has impacted my life and faith like raising my physically challenged daughter. Although I grieved for the child that wouldn't be, I was forever changed by the child that was. One frail little girl, unable to walk, dress herself, or even turn over at night, taught me more about God than all of the teachers and preachers I've ever known.

These lessons became mine in the triumphs and trials of her life. *God's strength is truly perfected in weakness*—hers and mine. The primary symptom of spinal muscular atrophy, Shela's disease, is muscle weakness. The wasting of her muscles resulted in extreme frailty. Shela had to have rods implanted to keep her spine straight and often needed to prop her head with her hands.

Yet Shela never focused on her cannots; she focused on her can-dos. And there were many. She read voraciously, memorized many Bible verses, and participated enthusiastically in children's choir. She also stenciled gift bags to give to friends and beaded salvation bracelets for the children's ministry at our church.

Shela was a daredevil. She dared to ride the wild rides with friends at amusement parks. She dared to go on youth trips without me. She even allowed "untrained" friends to take control of her wheelchair. And through it all, she smiled that delightful grin that assured startled observers all was right in Shela's world. She reminded us all that God's joy encounters no barriers and no limitations.

Mothering Shela in my weakness and God's strength taught me that His presence brings joy even in the most difficult circumstances.

It is possible to be content in any situation. I was shocked and thankful one day to hear Shela, as a preschooler, singing "I'm glad to be me." Incredible—unable to walk, crawl, or dress herself, Shela was glad to be who she was.

Shela was placed in our home for short term foster care as a four-month-old infant. When we gained permanent custody, we decided to retain her given name when we adopted her.

Later, I learned that Shela's name means "contented heart."
God's character within her demonstrated acceptance and peace
with the limitations of her body.

Once in a college essay, Shela wrote, "I would love to have
been a dancer." Instead she went to the recitals of a young friend
and experienced the vicarious delight of someone else's music and
movement. Much of Shela's contentment came from her unique
ability to feel another person's joy.

It was hard for me to rage against the difficulties of my life
when my own child calmly accepted her challenges with so much
grace. And it was harder still to resent others when Shela found so
many reasons to love them.

Servanthood can be embraced as a growth opportunity. While
caring for Shela and her four younger brothers, I also met the
needs of my elderly grandmother. When Grandmother turned
ninety, we brought her into our home.

Sometimes the workload seemed tremendous and the weariness
overwhelming. I often felt despair at the never-ending tasks. Isaiah
40:29 says, "He gives strength to the weary." I learned to run to God
for supernatural stamina.

In my role as a servant, I also learned to yield my rights and needs to Him. I clearly remember walking in my neighborhood one evening and crying out, "God, if my only purpose on this earth is to meet the needs of Shela and Grandmother, help me accept that. But I need Your grace to do it well."

Courage counts. At Shela's memorial service, our pastor said, "Perhaps the word that most clearly summarizes Shela Kirkpatrick's life is courage."

What was brave about Shela? Besides her commitment to living life, the clearest indication of her courage was seen in her response to personal crisis. Her greatest challenge came as a seventh grader when her wheelchair slipped off a steep sidewalk and her head took the force of the blow as the 100-pound chair slammed into the asphalt. She was rushed to the hospital to receive treatment for a traumatic brain injury.

The surgeon informed us, "The fall pulverized a portion of Shela's brain. We had to remove part of the left hemisphere. I don't know if she'll survive or what the results will be."

Through prayer, God's grace, and Shela's fighting spirit, she conquered surgery, the respirator, and pneumonia to leave the hospital in three weeks. The same doctor concluded, "This child miraculously survived. I am exceedingly well pleased."

On our own strength, we're completely inadequate in the face of our child's suffering. But with God's strength, how unbelievably strong we can be. In the hardest times of sickness and heartache, I sometimes wanted to flee. The responsibility for choices and the helplessness to change circumstances were overwhelming.

When we had to learn respiratory therapy to suction fluid from Shela's lungs and a "thumping" technique to loosen the mucous, I panicked. When I lived between hospital and home, I sometimes didn't want to get on the elevator.

Sometimes when Shela couldn't swallow well, anxiety would smother me, and I would find myself consumed with fear and self-doubt about my ability to meet her needs.

But then God would whisper, "Be still and know I am God"; "Do not be anxious about anything"; "I will strengthen you and help you" (Psalm 46:10, Philippians 4:4, Isaiah 41:10). I would go on. I'm so glad I didn't flee.

Shela's nineteen years on earth taught me things that are very much a part of who I am today. God called Shela home on a warm day ten years ago, and in the ensuing grief, I learned even more. After the raging pain ebbed, my faith and hope came to an even deeper place.

Perhaps the greatest gift came from God's assurance that

Shela is content and delighting in His presence. As the first Christmas after her death approached, I didn't know how to face a holiday forever changed.

A friend gave me a small package for Christmas, and I sat in Shela's room to open it. My tears flowed as the wrapping paper yielded to a lovely ballerina angel. It was God's reminder that my child who had never walked, yet longed to be a dancer, now danced before the throne of her heavenly Father.

Ecclesiastes 3:4 tells us that there is "a time to mourn and a time to dance." My daughter—my teacher—dances now. ⬡

My flesh and my heart may fail,
but God is the strength of my heart
and my portion forever.

PSALM 73:26

Cast Your Burdens

What are the biggest challenges facing you as a mother? Exhaustion? Discipline problems? Tough decisions?

Write out your biggest worries on small slips of paper and place them in a jar, praying over each. Then set the jar on your nightstand as a visual reminder to daily give God your worries and cares, knowing that He cares more for you and can do more through you than you ever thought possible.

Just as there comes a warm sunbeam
into every cottage window, so comes a love
born of God's care for every separate need.

NATHANIEL HAWTHORNE

A Ray of Sunshine

CINDY L. HEFLIN

I sat in silence by the kitchen window as autumn leaves tumbled in the early morning drizzle. The damp, dreary scene outside reflected the malignant despair in my soul. I sipped a steaming cup of tea and scanned the overcast skies, searching for a glimpse of sunshine. While my children slept, I lingered alone, deep in thought. Though I longed to feel the warmth of God's presence, my hot cup of tea did little to change the climate of my numb heart.

"Lord, I need Your help," I whispered, "and a ray of sunshine to pierce the clouds of my despair."

Several weeks had passed, but it seemed like only yesterday since the car accident on that sultry summer afternoon, and the ophthalmology exam that followed. Nothing could have prepared me for the doctor's devastating report, and his words still hammered in my memory— "severe retinal deterioration...loss of all peripheral vision...visual fields reduced to less than twenty degrees...never drive again."

Due to the severity of this loss, I was now legally blind.

Each day, those words haunted me and overshadowed my life, slamming the brakes on my independence. It crushed me to face my loss, my limitations, and the reality of the incurable disease slowly stealing my sight.

The children's playful chatter suddenly silenced my thoughts. Another day had begun. I muddled through a typical morning of breakfast, laundry, and Play-Doh, struggling to understand why God had allowed this to happen?

Despite my anxiety, I knew He would take care of our needs. But how? My husband often traveled out-of-state—for days, sometimes weeks at a time. I was used to being on the go, shuttling our girls to preschool, play-dates, and the pediatrician. I relished our spur-of-the-moment trips to visit out-of-town friends.

All of that was coming to an end. The challenge of my visual limitations overwhelmed me, and unwilling to burden others, I felt uncomfortable asking for help. It seemed impossible to cope with these sudden changes, even with God's help.

The telephone rang as I collapsed on the couch, weary from a long afternoon and a heavy heart. To my surprise, the friendly caller was Mary, a young mom from our church. Despite our mutual friends, we'd never met. With compassion, she expressed her concern for my family and me. "You know, I'm always out with my two kids. I'd really love the company if you ever need a ride." Within moments, we were making arrangements to run errands together one day each week.

A tear slipped down my cheek. I hung up the phone, feeling amazed and grateful. God had heard my feeble prayer and faithfully answered. A tiny seed of hope began to grow in my heart. After baths and bedtime stories, I kissed my girls goodnight, and then fell into bed exhausted, but with a new sense of peace. I thanked the Lord for meeting our need.

But what I didn't realize was that God was providing for more than just my need for transportation.

Mary arrived promptly the next afternoon. Her bright smile and cheerful nature were as sunny as her buttercup-yellow sedan. Each Tuesday, with the children buckled securely and the car stocked with plenty of books and snacks, we set out for an afternoon on the road. Soon I realized that traveling with Mary was more than just a trip to the bank, drugstore, or post office—it was fun. With games and songs, she entertained the children as we made our rounds "all through the town." Her joy and laughter were healing to my weary soul.

A road trip with Mary always included lively conversation that made my day better—and encouraged me to seek the Lord for the strength to overcome every trial.

Mary had a joy for the Lord I'd never seen or experienced. Something about her faith sparked my own desire to know God better. Being stripped of my wheels forced me to realign my priorities. I had to learn to put God first, study His Word, and surrender my pain to Him in prayer.

Before long, icy winds whistled through the barren branches that stretched across the winter sky. Housebound against my will, I felt shrouded in isolation like a tulip bulb trapped beneath the frozen ground. But a snowy afternoon spent at Mary's inviting home always cured my cabin fever. Over a cup of hot chocolate, we talked and laughed while our toddlers napped and the five-year-olds played board games on the floor nearby.

As I shared the strain these challenges were placing on my life, Mary listened patiently. "In seasons of joy or pain, always remember: God's love for you is greater than you can ever imagine," she encouraged. "We're all someone special in His eyes!"

The truth of her simple words shot straight into my heart, compelling me to keep trusting my Father. My faith began to flourish as I pulled the weeds of discouragement stunting its growth.

Soon the scent of apple blossoms and the welcome sunshine of spring revealed a new hope in my heart. In addition to our weekly trip, Mary often invited us to the playground or a picnic in the park. It felt wonderful to enjoying these simple pleasures with my girls once more. My despair softly subsided and my faith strengthened as I learned to focus on the Lord's faithfulness and compassion instead of my circumstances.

Adjusting to my loss of independence was difficult, but over time, I learned that God is always in control. "If it's God's will—God will provide a way," I reminded myself whenever an appointment or a special activity was planned and I wasn't quite sure how I would get us there. To this day, He's never left us stranded.

Though I continue to live with ever-increasing visual limitations, I strive to walk by faith, not by sight. For during my darkest days, He "who is able to do immeasurably more than all we ask or imagine" (Ephesians 3:20) provided for all my needs—and beyond. The shining light of the Lord's unfailing love transformed my heart, enabling me to see clearly that I can overcome any weakness when I place my faith in Him. ⬡

> *We wait in hope for the LORD;*
> *he is our help and our shield.*
> *In him our hearts rejoice*
> *for we trust in his holy name.*
> *May your unfailing love rest upon us, O LORD,*
> *even as we put our hope in you.*

PSALM 33:20-22

Dear Heavenly Father,

I'm overwhelmed today. There's so much to do, and I just don't feel like I have anything left to offer.

Lord, thank You that You invite me to cast my burdens on You. Thank You for the strength You give for each of the challenges that face me today. Thank You for being near.

Today, I pray for renewed strength and faith that You will help me meet my challenges, as well as wisdom to know what's most important. Thank You for Your grace.

The hardest part of raising
a child is teaching them to ride bicycles.
A shaky child on a bicycle for the first time
needs both support and freedom.
The realization that this is what
the child will always need can hit hard.

SLOAN WILSON

Letting Go

It's not easy to think about the day our kids will leave the nest. The truth is that they leave the nest a little every day, and those little moments of increasing independence are a strange mixture of pride, joy, and a sweet sadness. No matter how big our kids get, though, they'll always need a mother's love.

There is a time for everything, and
a season for every activity under heaven.

ECCLESIASTES 3:1

It will be gone before you know it.
The fingerprints on the wall appear
higher and higher. Then
suddenly they disappear.

DOROTHY EVSLIN

From My Son

JOAN CLAYTON

"Look, Mom! He followed me all the way home from school.
Isn't he cute? Can I keep him? He won't eat very much, and I
promise I'll be the one who feeds him!"

"You know what, Mom? You're the best mom in the whole
world. Will you marry me when I grow up?"

"Guess what, Mom? The teacher asked me to bring the cookies
for the Christmas party. Can I help you roll them out? Yeah, I've
been playing with the dog, but I didn't get my hands dirty."

"Guess what, Mom? It took me five years, three months, and
two days, but I finally made 'good citizen' in my class."

"Hey, Mom, guess what? There's a girl in sixth grade who says
she likes me better than any other boy in the whole school. She
said we were 'going together' until further notice. Well, yeah, I
guess I like her—she told me I did, anyway."

"But, Mom, don't you know all the kids date now? Why do I
have to wait until I'm sixteen? That's dumb. Wait—you mean
you'll have to drive us and be with us the whole time? Well, never

mind. I didn't really want to go anyway."

"Guess what Mom? You'll never believe it. I got the John Phillip Sousa Award in band. Yes, Mom, I know you're proud of me."

"You know what, Mom? I really don't think I'm ready for college yet. I think I'll just live at home and get a job. Anyway, I'd miss the peanut butter fudge at Christmastime."

"Mom, now that I'm nineteen, I feel like I really need to get out on my own and move away. Don't cry—you've been the most wonderful mom in the whole world, but I think it's time for me to grow up."

"Well, Mom, I got a job. It doesn't pay a whole lot, but it's a good job. Don't worry—I'm just a two-hour drive away. By the way, you know that leather coat of mine that Dad liked on me? Do you think I could sell it to him?"

"Guess what, Mom? I've enrolled in some night classes. I knew you'd be happy. Yes, I am hoping to graduate someday. No, you don't have to help. Yes, I'm eating right. No, I don't eat a candy bar for breakfast—well, not every day, anyway."

"Hi, Mom. Graduation is Saturday afternoon at two o'clock. Yes, I know how proud you and Dad are of me. Oh, and Mom, I've invited a friend to graduation. And would you please not even bring up her blue eyes and blonde hair? I know I always said I didn't like blue eyes and blonde hair, but this one is different!"

"Hey, Mom. I thought you would never answer the phone! So what are you and Dad doing November 19? Would you like to go to a wedding?"

"She's the most wonderful girl, Mom. She's the girl I've been looking for all my life. You're really going to love her. Remember all those bedtime prayers? The thousands of times you prayed for the girl who would someday be my wife? Well, I think your prayers have been answered!

And guess what, Mom? I love you!"

"Oh, and hey—happy Mother's Day!" ⬡

We always thank God for you, as is right,
for we are thankful that your faith is flourishing and
you are all growing in love for each other.

2 THESSALONIANS 1:3 NLT

Cherished Traditions

NANCY B. GIBBS

The first day of school was always a happy time for Grace. While her kids were getting ready for school, she would move throughout the house singing "School Days" for their amusement. It became a favorite family tradition. The first day of her oldest son's senior year, however, was bittersweet. She knew this would be the last time she would sing the tune to Brett.

One year later, the telephone rang the night before her son's first day of college classes. "Hi, Mom," Brett began. They talked briefly about what the next day held. And then, just before they hung up, Brett ventured to ask the real question on his mind: "Mom, are you going to call me to sing 'School Days' tomorrow morning?"

Bright and early the next day, Brett—and a few of his new friends—laughed as Grace sang a very familiar song. Smiling, she hung up as she brushed away a few happy tears.

Tradition is a form of promise
from parent to child.
It's a way to say, "I love you,
I'm here for you, and some
things will not change."

LYNN LUDWICK

Even though your kids may not be paying attention,
you have to pay attention to them. And with
the attention, of course, must be all the love you
can give. Then, when the kids start doing
strange things under the guise of independence,
they will always know that they are loved
and that the lines are always open for them
to send a message back to earth.

BILL COSBY

I prayed for this child,
and the LORD has granted me
what I asked of him. So now
I give him to the LORD.
For his whole life he will
be given over to the LORD.

1 SAMUEL 1:27-28

Training Wheels

It's not always easy to accept our kids' independence. Maybe a good place to start is to give them a few choices and an opportunity to spread their wings. This week, help your child pick out an age-appropriate hobby, something he or she really wants to do. Once you've gotten the ball rolling, allow your child to take personal responsibility for the tasks involved with his or her new hobby, and be ready with some words of encouragement.

The pangs you feel as they gain independence will be overshadowed by the joy of seeing them grow.

*Commit everything
you do to the Lord. Trust him,
and he will help you.*

Psalm 37:5 NLT

It's not only children who grow.
Parents do too. As much
as we watch to see what our children
do with their lives, they are
watching us to see what we do
with ours. I can't tell my children
to reach for the sun.
All I can do is reach for it, myself.

JOYCE MAYNARD

God's Plan for Me

GLORIA CASSITY STARGEL

"What's the matter?" my husband, Joe, asked one night as we sat at the dinner table.

"Well," I sighed, "it's only a matter of months before all the boys are out of the house. I guess I'm suffering from empty nest syndrome." What would I do now that Joe was retired and I didn't have the boys to keep up with anymore? Their absence would leave a huge void in my day, not to mention my sense of having something meaningful to do.

"Why don't you go back to school?"

His suggestion stunned me. "Do you realize it's been twenty-seven years since I was a student?"

But maybe, I thought, I should be more open to the idea. A year earlier I had faced Joe's life-threatening illness. Always a planner, a perfectionist, and a procrastinator, with Joe in the hospital and the world crumbling at my feet, I saw the futility of my so carefully laid plans. I had to learn to trust God, and I grew to earnestly want to trust Him in all areas of my life. I wanted to find His will for me and to do it. And if His will was for me to go back to school, I would.

But first I had to know who I was—to find me. In the words
of Saint Augustine, "Let me know Thee, Lord, and let me know
myself." As I prayed for guidance and started to consider where
I'd been and where I wanted to go, the idea of going back to school
began to burrow in my heart. And then, with fear and trembling, I
returned to Brenau College, a first-quarter sophomore. "Please,
Lord, don't leave me now."

Unexpectedly, college became a spiritual experience, one that
changed my life and gave me the inner security I craved. The key, I
think, was obedience.

My obedience was tested during my junior year when I felt
like God was directing me to study journalism. For several months
I doggedly continued social work studies, despite the divine pull I
felt toward the English department. Surely I had imagined God's
message. What would I do with journalism?

But He didn't give up on me, and I'm so grateful. I felt no
peace until I went to my knees in surrender and changed my major
field of study.   For years I had known Jesus as my Savior; now I
accepted Him as my Lord. I thought I was really sacrificing by
surrendering my desires, but to my surprise and delight, it was my
gain. When I gave Him the old insecure me and surrendered to

His plans, He gave me a freedom I had never known.

It seemed the more I gave up my will to God's will, the more I felt the presence of the Holy Spirit. And one of the first and most important things the Spirit taught me was that God loves me. Now if God loves me, that makes me somebody rather special. I don't need to question who I am anymore. I'm a child of the King! What a freeing revelation—freeing me from the chains of my own self-doubts.

Now I understood the reason for my studying journalism. God wanted me to write for Him, to tell others He loves them, too.

And that's what I do now. Writing for Christian magazines and books brings me peace and happiness, knowing I'm fulfilling God's plan for my life, Phase Two, post motherhood. I've seen His hand in my life through my years as a mother, and I continue to feel the rushing wind of His loving guidance as I journey with Him into the future. ⬡

> *Trust in the* Lord *with all your heart,*
> *and lean not on your own understanding;*
> *in all your ways acknowledge him,*
> *and he will make your paths straight.*
>
> Proverbs 3:5-6

Dear Heavenly Father,

My kids are growing up so fast. And I know I need to let them conquer their challenges, but sometimes it's so tempting to step in and do everything for them, to shield them from pain or trouble. Lord, please give me wisdom to do what's best for my kids, and to know when to jump in and when to step aside.

And Father, thank You so much for being such a wonderful Father, for loving me so tenderly. Please comfort my heart when it hurts to let go, Lord. I'm so grateful for Your loving hand in my life.

Becoming a grandmother is wonderful.
One moment you're just a mother.
The next you are all-wise and prehistoric.

PAM BROWN

Becoming a Grandma

Who knew this day would be so amazing? Now that the kids are grown and starting families of their own, you get to experience anew all the fun of having a little one in the house—the tiny clothes, the first words, the smell of baby shampoo. And this time around, you get to be "Grandma," the source of candy bars and hugs. What better reward could a mother receive?

Children's children are a crown to the aged,
and parents are the pride of their children.

PROVERBS 17:6

It's such a grand thing to be a mother
of a mother—that's why the world
calls her grandmother.

AUTHOR UNKNOWN

My Trip to Grandmotherhood

EMILY TIPTON WILLIAMS

The first Sunday of December dawned chilly, but not cold, in Fort Worth, Texas. I sat in the violin section with sixty plus musicians surrounding me, while the massive choir of the Broadway Baptist Church stood on risers behind the orchestra. Last-minute arrivals scurried in to find a seat.

The somber notes of the overture began. I thought of the countless times I had performed this music, but I never tire of Handel's genius blending of composition and scripture. Music filled the sanctuary, and swelled to a new height when the audience joined in with the choir.

This was the twentieth performance of the *Messiah* sing-along at this church. As I played and listened to the flowing voice of the lyric soprano singing "I Know That My Redeemer Liveth," I thought of the busy week ahead in preparation for my trip to New York City. My daughter, Jennifer, was expecting my first grandchild.

The time whizzed by, as it often does when I'm performing. As usual, I experienced the same thrill as my fingers danced over the strings playing the Halleluiah Chorus. The audience stood as they sang with the chorus and orchestra. As we packed up our instruments, musician friends wished me well on my trip to grandmotherhood.

After arriving home and drinking a cup of hot chocolate, I fell peacefully asleep. At 3:00 A.M., my husband answered the jangling phone. "What? Are you sure?" He handed me the phone. My heart pounded.

"Mom, I'm in labor."

"You can't be, not until next week."

"We're on the way to the hospital. Matt will call."

"I'll be there as soon as I can. I love you."

"I love you, Mom."

I started packing just in case. Probably false labor pains, I kept telling myself. When I checked, the early morning flights were all crowded. What would you expect the Monday after Thanksgiving?

Another call. "Mom, it's the real thing," Jennifer said calmly. I wasn't a bit calm.

Now it was just before 6:00 A.M, and I was waiting at a gate at the airport, hoping for available space. As I kept in contact with my daughter and son-in-law on cell phones, I was turned away again and again. I hurried from one gate to the next.

By noon, I sat reading a Susan Howatch novel in a waiting area. A woman sitting across from me spoke. "I enjoy her books too. Haven't read that one."

We visited a while. She was a chaplain at a university in Oklahoma. When I told her of my predicament, she responded, "I'll pray for you." We separated and I headed for another gate. When I arrived, I noticed a sign propped up on the counter: "No Space Available." I said a quick prayer and walked up to the gate agent. She looked up from her computer.

"I can read, but I have a problem. My daughter is in labor in New York City."

"There is no way you'll get on a plane today," she said in a tone of total disinterest. "Why don't you go back home and fly up tomorrow?"

"I can't. This is my first grandbaby, and I have to be there."

"It would take a miracle for you to get to New York City today," she responded.

I looked her straight in the eye. "I believe in miracles."

She stared at me and gave a nod. "Go sit over there."

I watched as she tapped, tapped, tapped on the keyboard as though playing an intricate Bach fugue. After a few minutes she walked over and handed me a boarding pass. "Don't tell anyone," she whispered.

I've never been so happy to sit in the middle seat on the back row of an airplane in all my life. I called New York and reported my success.

"Hurry," said Matt. "Come to the hospital as soon as you land."

LaGuardia Airport. The taxi line snaked up and down at least four times. I heard a man say that the delay was up to two hours.

I had no choice but to join the line. After a few minutes, a man dressed in a driver's uniform walked up. "I've got a limousine. If I get enough people at fifty dollars each, I can take you to the city immediately."

You should have seen me, a Texan, offering limo rides to strangers. As soon as eight of us were loaded into the car, I told my story, and the New Yorkers unanimously agreed I should be dropped off first at New York Presbyterian Hospital.

I arrived just in time. Aidan was born later that evening. When I held my grandbaby in my arms for the first time, my heart soared with the words of an Italian proverb, "When a baby is born, so is a grandmother." ⬡

I will be glad and rejoice in you;
I will sing praise to your name, O Most High.

PSALM 9:2

What a wonderful contribution
our grandmothers and grandfathers
can make if they will share some
of the rich experiences and their
testimonies with their children
and grandchildren.

VAUGHN J. FEATHERSTONE

Raising a Happy Parent

NANCY B. GIBBS

"Mama, my baby has a heart," Chad proclaimed over the telephone. "Lucy and I just left the doctor's office. We heard the baby's heartbeat. I just couldn't believe it!"

Chad's mother grinned. She thought back twenty-eight years earlier to the day she first heard his heartbeat. The sound was music to her ears and brought joy to her heart. She understood the parental instincts her son was feeling.

She looked forward to the day that his baby—her grandbaby—would come into the world. By the tone of his voice she knew that one day soon, as a parent, her son would better understand that, as parents, our hearts are the happiest when they are beating for our children. Something that won't change over twenty-eight years or a lifetime. ⬡

Mothers are angels
who teach their children to fly.

AUTHOR UNKNOWN

Love from Grandma

What makes a grandma so great is the way she lavishes love on her grandkids. What can you do this week to give your grandkids that feeling of being loved, nurtured, and supported? Maybe a trip to the zoo? (Your kids would probably appreciate that!) Maybe a scrapbook of fun things you've done together? Simply a phone call, or baking cookies together? However you show it, take joy in your grandkids today.

Sharing time together is a precious gift
of love and trust that each family member gives
to the others. A strong sense of family unity,
belonging, and warmth doesn't just happen.
It is nurtured and grown over time,
just as a lovely garden flourishes in the
hands of a caring, diligent gardener.

RICHARD PATTERSON, JR.

Grandchildren are the dots
that connect the lines from
generation to generation.

LOIS WYSE

The First Noel—in My Family

NANETTE THORSEN-SNIPES

This Christmas brought my family more gifts, more love, and more joy than ever before—it brought my first granddaughter.

When the call came on December 23, my husband and I drove like mad to the hospital in Alabama where the little one lay wrapped in a fuzzy blanket cocoon. My daughter-in-law, Jennifer, had a Caesarean, but both she and the baby—a saucy little girl— made it through with no complications.

Standing at the glass partition, my husband and I watched the nurse bring Catie Noel into the room, clean out her mouth, then bathe her and shampoo her black curls. The nurse then wrapped our squalling infant and lifted her for us to see.

"Jim," I said, "she looks just like me!"

Catie Noel was beautiful. Her jet-black hair clung to her head in tiny ringlets. It didn't matter that she had a blotchy red face and her eyes were swollen—I instantly recognized her as one of my own.

Nudging my husband, I said aloud to anyone standing near,

"She looks just like my side of the family."

"Does it really matter?" a nurse standing next to me asked.

Of course it did, I thought. This was my first granddaughter and she looked just like me.

Later in the hospital room, the other grandmother and I took turns holding my granddaughter. "You know," Jennifer's mother said, giving the baby a pacifier, "her mouth is shaped like our side of the family." She placed a red bow in Catie Noel's black hair. "Yes, and her hair looks just like mine used to."

I couldn't believe what I was hearing. Anyone could see that Catie Noel was the spitting image of me.

Soon it was time to go home, and for the next month, I hummed, "My First Noel."

Some time later, Jennifer and Donnie brought Catie and her older brother, Cayson, to visit. With all of them by my side, I took the opportunity to dig through dusty photo albums looking for a picture to prove that Catie looked like my side of the family.

I was thrilled to find my son's birth wristband buried between the pages. I dug further and found a yellowing "Mother's Instruction Sheet," which my first pediatrician sent home with new mothers.

Jennifer held it and an impish grin lit up her face. "You mean you got an instruction sheet with your baby?" Incredulously, she surveyed my son, then shot a look at me. "Are you sure you read the whole thing?"

Just then, Catie let out a loud protest. Closing the photo album and the chapter on who favored whom, I picked up my granddaughter and kissed her cheek. It no longer mattered who she looked like—she was simply Catie Noel. And she belonged to all of us. ⬡

But from everlasting to everlasting
the Lord's love is with those who fear him,
and his righteousness with their children's children.

PSALM 103:17

Dear Heavenly Father,

I can't believe this day is here—I'm a grandma! Thank You, Lord, for the joy of seeing my children grow up to have children of their own.

Lord, today I ask You for special strength to lead my grandchildren to know You. I want to pass along a heritage of faith, and I pray that my grandkids would see You in my life. And I want so much to be a source of strength and support for my kids and grandkids—please give me extra love to spread among my family and wisdom to know when to hold my tongue.

Lord, thank You for this wonderful day.

Whenever I held my
newborn baby in my arms,
I used to think that what I said
and did to him could have
an influence not only on him
but on all whom he met, not
only for a day or a month
or a year, but for all eternity—
a very challenging and exciting
thought for a mother.

ROSE KENNEDY

A Mother Matters

Sometimes we want what's best for our kids so badly and take our caring role in their lives so seriously that we can't bear to think of failing even a little. But, really, our kids need us, imperfections and all. Even on our worst days, we are an essential force of love in their lives.

Train a child in the way he should go,
and when he is old he will not turn from it.

PROVERBS 22:6

Mother love is the fuel that enables
a normal human being to do the impossible.

MARION C. GARRETTY

She Still Teaches Me

JERRY D. LANE

My mother was my first teacher. I learned all kinds of things from her, from Bible verses to how to peel carrots to the proper use of "me" and "I." Both my mom and my dad taught me about faith—I remember our nightly prayer times like they happened yesterday. I guess I'm used to thinking of only my high school teachers and college professors as real teachers, but I've come to realize that my mom is a teacher for life in every sense of the word.

I was raised in a Christian home, and while we had our share of troubles just like every family, nothing in my background could have prepared my family for what I put them through one summer a few years ago. They were all shocked by the rapid downward spiral that took me from being an all-around easygoing guy to attempting suicide in a matter of months. The ensuing hospital stay and the years that followed were horrifically difficult. And while no one can feel what someone else feels or know the pain of another person, I think a mother has a unique understanding of her child's pain. My mom was no exception. She hurt with me—deeply.

For nearly three years after the suicide attempt, I experienced some good times, but most of the time I was just barely making it. At one point, I started doing better spiritually, physically, emotionally, and financially—but then things fell apart again. I became paralyzed, not physically, even though it sometimes felt like it, but emotionally. I couldn't move or get out of bed. I cried for hours each day. I began secretly stockpiling pills again, and night after night I fought the urge to escape the darkness that was now my life by ending it. Hopelessness had set in and seemed insistent on staying.

Desperate, I decided to share this raging war with my mom. It wasn't easy to get the words out. I'm sure it was a living nightmare for her to hear again. But, just as she had done my entire life, she put her feelings aside and stayed right there with me. She'd been my combat buddy throughout this whole ordeal, and she wasn't going anywhere.

I still felt alone in the fight a lot of the time. One night when I was home visiting, my mom, knowing that nighttime was the hardest time for me, asked if we could pray together before I went to bed. So we began praying that night, acknowledging God's presence and power and asking for His help together.

A few days later, after driving to my home in Dallas, I called Mom. When we'd finished chatting, she asked if she could pray with me again. And so began a nightly routine that I found to be a powerful time of reconnecting with God, with her, and with others. In the past years, I had withdrawn and become reclusive out of the depression, but as my mom and I prayed, God began healing me. It didn't happen in an instant; it was the persistence of our phone-call prayers. After a few months, light started shining in my heart once again, and I felt more able to face the day and to connect with people.

By praying with me, my mom taught me that God was still there, even though I couldn't feel His presence. She taught me to cry out to God, just as David cried out to God in the midst of darkness and fear. She also taught me something beautiful and amazing: that I wasn't alone. Jesus was with me just as He promised, and my mom was with me even if only by phone.

My mom and I have a completely different, and much closer, relationship than we did before my depression. We share the highs and the lows, and we cry out to God together. Her faithfulness to me mirrors God's faithfulness—my doctors are amazed by how much progress I've made.

I've learned a lot from my mom—about commitment, faithful prayer, childlike faith, and how to be close to people. I think, in a very real way, she saved my life. If she hadn't been the committed teacher and friend that she was, I'm not sure where I'd be. Only a mother can be such a powerful teacher. ⬡

Love never gives up,
never loses faith,
is always hopeful,
and endures through
every circumstance.

1 Corinthians 13:7 NLT

Not in Vain

EMILY DICKINSON

If I can stop one heart from breaking,
I shall not live in vain:
If I can ease one life the aching,
Or cool one pain,
Or help one fainting robin
Unto his nest again,
I shall not live in vain.

In My Steps

NANCY B. GIBBS

My four-year-old was on my heels no matter where I went. Whenever I stopped to do something and turned back around, I would trip over him.

I patiently suggested fun activities to keep him occupied. But he simply smiled an innocent smile and said, "Oh, that's all right, Mommy. I'd rather be in here with you." Then he continued to bounce happily along behind me.

After stepping on his toes for the fifth time, I began to lose patience.

When I asked him why he was acting this way, he looked up at me with sweet green eyes and said, "Well, Mommy, my Sunday school teacher told me to walk in Jesus' footsteps. I can't see Him, so I'm walking in yours!" ⬡

Mother is the name
for God in the lips and hearts
of little children.

WILLIAM MAKEPEACE THACKERAY

Sabbath Rest

A mother's work is never done. Fortunately, it can be
paused. Take a break this weekend—arrange for a little
babysitting help for an hour or two (or three or four) and
spend some time relaxing. Grab some dessert with
girlfriends, or just relax with a good book. Take the time
to refresh your spirit, and remember that you're important
and doing important work. ⬡

*Charm is deceptive,
and beauty is fleeting;
but a woman who fears
the LORD is to be praised.*

PROVERBS 31:30

There is no way to be a perfect mother,
and a million ways to be a good one.

JILL CHURCHILL

Confessions of an Imperfect Mom

LETTIE KIRKPATRICK BURRESS

Having long lived with a burden of guilt and desperately needing to do penance, I have decided to go public. It is time to share with other struggling moms some of my more glaring inadequacies. Perhaps realizing that four of my children are boys will cause some degree of grace to be extended.

The following list is only a beginning. A sequel may be offered if the demand is great.

- I did not bathe my babies every day (they were simply too slippery). And I discovered that baby lotions are great tools for concealing such "neglect."
- My kids don't always "match"—sometimes not even their shoes. I had a three-year-old who was known for his eccentric personality, a reputation verified by the mismatched cowboy boots he wore on most outings. These were later replaced by a pair he picked out for fifty cents at a yard sale.

- My boys sleep on the floor—a lot. I don't know if this is poor child rearing, but it certainly seems rather primitive. Add to this the revelation that they also sleep in their clothes frequently (mostly sweats, seldom ties and sport coats) and I am a sure candidate for stern reprimand.

- We don't have a "family dinner" every evening, or even many evenings. I acknowledge that this brings frowns to the faces of family experts, and it is with great grief that I reveal it. I simply have not been able to gather the kids and my husband (who has a lengthy commute) from all corners of the school grounds, ballparks, and job locations.

  Does it count to come together on Sundays at Pizza Hut, as well as all the major holidays, birthdays, and large family gatherings? Do we get any credit for meeting around the oven as we prepare our plates in shifts?

- Our family devotions can get ugly. The most striking example of this confession occurred one Thanksgiving (during a family mealtime, I'd like to point out). I had lovingly prepared personal placecards inscribed with Bible verses, and made photocopies of seasonal praise choruses for us to sing together. We would then share intimate expressions of gratitude with each other over the steaming gravy boat.

However, as the three-year-old had recently crumpled my lovely leaf-shaped napkins, placing one in each plate, and my thirteen-year-old was outraged that we were condescending to having turkey breast instead of a whole turkey, the mood was grim. I don't recall ever hearing a surlier version of "Thank You, Lord." It was the stuff memories are made of.

- I sometimes abandon ship, give up the battle, throw in the towel, concede defeat, or all of the above. Despite my best efforts, between toddlers, teens, tweens, and college geniuses, as well as hormones, spitballs, male aggression, and a sometimes oblivious hubby, sometimes bailing out is the best option other than screaming.

Once the decision to abandon ship has been made, I grab my car keys and a good book and drive to the parking lot of the nearest grocery store. There, in blessed "solitude," I let God restore my soul. It isn't admirable, but it's survival.

There is a brighter side to these failures and the multitude of others I've "neglected" to mention: God has told us He knows that we are but flesh and He is our Redeemer. This is, thankfully, also true for our parenting goofs.

These same children who have gone unbathed, slept on the floor, hurled mashed potatoes during a rare family mealtime, received "mixed" spiritual counsel, and been abandoned when they should have been controlled have reminded me of great truths about God's redemptive nature.

- Three of my four sons have wanted to marry me. The youngest just isn't old enough to propose yet.
- My teenage daughter, for all of her resistance to Mom's harebrained holiday ideas, once wrote a school essay indicating that I was her best friend.
- One child gave his testimony at church and shared that his mom loved him more than anything and had introduced him to Jesus.
- My five-year-old said I was the prettiest mom he knew (I know— time for an eye exam).
- My oldest son asks me to pray with him.

- Following the disastrous Thanksgiving devotional, there was a note on my dresser. My ten-year-old wanted us to know he thanked God for his parents.

The conclusion of my conscience cleansing? Not that we should excuse our failures, if that's what they really are. But let's grant to ourselves the magnificent grace of the God who redeems. ⬡

I will tell of the LORD's unfailing love.
I will praise the LORD for all he has done.

Isaiah 63:7 NLT

The woman who creates
and sustains a home,
and under whose hands children
grow up to be strong and
pure men and women, is a creator
second only to God.

HELEN HUNT JACKSON

Light from Mother's Lamp

STAN MEEK

Missionary E. Stanley Jones tells of a "wonderful old brass lamp" in an ancient church in India. The lamp had many arms hanging from the ceiling, and at the end of each arm a cup with oil and a wick. At the close of a service, young people would take a wick from the lamp to guide the people home through the night. It was a beautiful sight to watch the flickering points of light moving through the darkness, illuminating the rough path trod by seekers of truth.

I barely remember the coal oil lamps that illuminated our simple farm structure nestled in the red hills of the Cimarron Valley. Compared with today's electric lights, those early lamps produced very little light, cast a lot of shadows, and were often very smelly. But there was another lamp in our home—a lamp that gave my soul illumination, cast no shadows, and left a sweet, lasting fragrance. It was the lamp of my mother's life.

By Mother's lamp, I first learned truthfulness. She expected truthfulness from her four boys, and her eyes could drag the truth right out of you.

By Mother's lamp I learned the tenderness of love. Some call it kindness, but it was more than the ordinary, vanilla kindness of practiced platitudes. It flowed from a deeper source. From Mother I learned to respect all persons long before multiculturalism became popular, to go the extra mile to protect or help someone else.

By Mother's lamp I learned that love can be severe as well as tender. Her love was not the wimpy, indulgent kind. It was love that cared enough to confront, correct, and even discipline when necessary. It was this severe love that taught me accountability and self-discipline.

Mother's lamp gave me an understanding of sacrificial love. Depression years dug deeply into my childhood, and while Mother had a natural affinity for aesthetics—things beautiful—she had few of those things. She went without pretty dresses and furniture so that her boys would have school clothes, books, and food on the table.

From Mother's cup of oil I took the wick of prayer. How vivid is the memory of her silhouette gliding silently past lightning-illuminated windows on stormy Oklahoma nights. We knew she was praying to keep her four boys safe.

From Mother's lamp I gained a reverence for the Bible. We were never to set anything on top of that leather-bound book in the living room. It was not legalism. It was simply a profoundly held respect for our daily Bread. No wonder then, when serving my country during the Korean War, I found myself turning to the Scriptures so often.

And it was from Mother's lamp that I received my first and best glimpse of holy living, of that special way of approaching life with reverence for the Lord and gratitude for His blessings.

In short, Mother, you lit the fire of faith in me. At times my own lamp has burned too dimly and smoked terribly compared to yours. But I desire to be a point of light against the night.

One of the evocative images of the past is that of the old lamplighter, ambling along the street spilling light on darkened street corners. We have no need today for the old streetlamp lighters—but show me a city, a home, or a heart that does not need a mother's lamp. ⬡

Listen, my son, to your father's instruction
and do not forsake your mother's teaching.
They will be a garland to grace your head
and a chain to adorn your neck.

PROVERBS 1:8-9

Dear Heavenly Father,

There are some days I feel so completely unappreciated. I do what I do because I love my family, but would it be so bad to have someone notice the sacrifices I make once in a while? And then there are some days when I wonder if what I do even makes a difference.

God, thank You that You understand what I'm going through, and that You lavish me with grace and understanding. Thank You that I don't have to be perfect to make a difference in my kids' lives. Thank You for Your wild, extravagant love—and for those little moments of reward that seem to come along just when I need them most.

All that I am or ever hope to be,
I owe to my angel Mother.

ABRAHAM LINCOLN

To Our Mothers

What would we do without our mothers? We certainly rely on Mom for advice about bottle temperature and how long to cook a pot roast. Maybe it's only after we've grown up and had kids of our own that we fully appreciate everything she did for us as kids, what she meant to our lives. The good news is it's never too late to say thank you.

Her children rise and call her blessed.

PROVERBS 31:28

Sweater, n.: garment worn
by child when its mother
is feeling chilly.

AMBROSE BIERCE

The Great Coverer

CANDY ARRINGTON

At some point when we were kids, we dubbed Mama "The Great Coverer." She seems to have some sort of internal drive to ensure the warmth and comfort of anyone within hugging distance. It is not unusual for a family member, friend, or stranger, reclining, even though briefly, to awake covered with an afghan, blanket, or an occasional beach towel. Mama's comfort-giving mechanism requires her to cover at every possible opportunity. For Mama, comfort-giving is synonymous with love.

Mama's covering isn't limited to those dozing. For years, she carried sweaters in the trunk of her car for my children. The trunk was most often popped and sweaters retrieved just before we entered a local restaurant that served frosty confections. As the children began to shiver while consuming their treats in air-conditioned comfort, the little sweaters appeared from her lap to swallow chill-bumped arms. To my knowledge those little sweaters still travel in her trunk—just in case. My kids are now in their teens.

When I was a child, we attended every Friday night high school football game. To my embarrassment, Mama always trailed into the stadium with scratchy wool army blankets in tow. As cheerleaders flipped, titans clashed, bands piped, and nippy autumn air swirled, Mama spread the woolen wraps around us and passed steaming cups of hot chocolate poured from a plaid thermos.

On one occasion, when the temperatures were well below freezing, she produced large plastic leaf bags and insisted we stand in them and cinch the drawstrings around our waists. One unsuspecting father and son in front of us came under her ministrations when she determined they were armed only with sweaters for the evening and insisted they don trash bags also. You can imagine the questioning looks from our stand-mates.

The county fair was a treat for us kids with its barns of animal smells, house of flowers, cotton candy hawkers, and glittering midway. I remember the swish of the corduroy pants Mama insisted I wear under my jumper to ward off chilly evening temper-atures. A sweater topped by a jacket, hat, and gloves completed the ensemble, and I was toasty warm for the evening's excitement.

Although Mama's covering efforts occasionally annoyed me, they were always done with the best intentions. Perhaps her desire to cover was a result of being the oldest of five children and feeling the need to take care of her siblings. Or possibly, the affects of the Great Depression left an indelible mark, nurturing Mama's natural inclination to meet other people's needs. Whatever the reasons, Mama never wants anyone to be uncomfortable.

God's love is similar to the Great Coverer's. His love enfolds us in a blanket of protection and encouragement when trouble and uncertainty blusters into our lives. His peace spreads comfort over all life's trials. The sin-cover of the blood of Jesus brings us into right standing with the Father and allows us to call Him Abba—"Daddy."

Somehow, I imagine when Mama enters heaven, God will be waiting, ready to swathe her in the embrace of His everlasting arms. And I wouldn't be surprised if the Great Coverer and the Great Comforter spend eternity in a never-ending hug. ⬡

He will cover you with his feathers,
and under his wings you will find refuge.

PSALM 91:4

Thanks, Mom

What do you most appreciate about your mom? What about her parenting do you most want to emulate? Take the time today to tell her. Write a letter of thanks and encouragement for the mark your mother left on your life.

*We always thank God
for you and pray
for you constantly.*

1 THESSALONIANS 1:2 NLT

The Name of Mother

FANNY CROSBY

The light, the spell-word of the heart,
Our guiding star in weal or woe,
Our talisman—our earthly chart—
That sweetest name that earth can know.

We breathed it first with lisping tongue
When cradled in her arms we lay;
Fond memories round that name are hung
That will not, cannot pass away.

We breathed it then, we breath it still,
More dear than sister, friend, or brother;
The gentle power, the magic thrill
Awakened by the name of Mother.

Honor your father and mother,
and love your neighbor as yourself.

MATTHEW 19:19

Each day of our lives
we make deposits in the
memory banks of our children.

CHARLES R. SWINDOLL

From Griping to Gratitude

GEORGIA RICHARDSON

Little did Mother know that something she designed as punishment would bring her children a lifetime of pleasure and aid them in solving life's little problems—or did she?

With five girls in our family, our childhood was full of excitement, to say the least, but we behaved ourselves most of the time. We would, however, cross the line every now and then. When this happened, we lost all privileges, normally for a two-week period: no telephone calls, TV, cruising on Sunday afternoons with the gang, and absolutely no dating. Mother meant business.

The one thing Mother did allow was working jigsaw puzzles. At first, this punishment stunned us. We called it downright cruel, inhuman, and boring. It served absolutely no purpose. Any idiot could work a jigsaw puzzle. How could she? And so we griped—and griped and griped.

Mother just listened to our cries of anguish, smiled, and then produced the worn card table equipped with one chair and one jigsaw puzzle. Surrendered to our fate, we lifted the lid on the box and began. She would stop by and try to make light conversation, but we ignored her completely. After all, she was the warden.

But we soon softened, and before long, two chairs appeared at the card table. Laughter followed, and one by one the other sisters would drop by. Extra chairs made their way to the table, and the floor opened for discussion: What were the big trends in clothes for fall? Who was going steady with whom? Boys, of course, always boys.

What we didn't realize was that while Mother was dealing with an immediate transgression, she was also learning about her children's lifestyles, friends, habits, and anything else a mother would want to know. She was molding our characters and teaching values that would last a lifetime. We never thought of our conversations as having secrets pried out of us by Mother, and it took years to realize that she had become not only our friend and confidant, but our very best friend. The puzzles were always completed, then scraped off the table and put away until the next offense was committed.

I can't remember a time when that rickety old card table wasn't set up in the living room. Not that we were continually in trouble. No, those conversation times became such a tradition that we kept a puzzle on the table year round. Instead of griping about forced fellowship with each other, we learned to feel gratitude for these opportunities. Broken hearts were mended, sibling rivalry was vented, and dreams were born. That old table in the corner became so popular that when our friends dropped by, they never left without working at least one piece and solving at least one problem.

After everyone left home, Mother removed the card table—but only temporarily. With an illness, a new grandchild, even Thanksgiving and Christmas celebrations, the card table—and a puzzle—reappeared.

Today, all five of us have card tables in our homes (each one a gift from Mother), and all of us keep a jigsaw puzzle either in the works or standing by, just waiting for one of our children to show a need to talk. Even our children's friends work them when they drop by, each of them sharing something personal, and each of them giving a little of themselves.

The other day, I ran into a friend I had not seen in years. We got to reminiscing about the old days, and he recalled, "I remember your family always had a jigsaw puzzle set up in the living room. I never understood what you all got out of working those crazy puzzles." I smiled to myself and thought, *You know, we didn't either, until now.*

Thanks, Mom. ⬡

I thank my God every time I remember you.

PHILIPPIANS 1:3

A good character is the best tombstone.
Those who loved you and were helped
by you will remember you when
forget-me-nots have withered.
Carve your name on hearts,
not on marble.

CHARLES H. SPURGEON

My Mother's Legacy

LEANN CAMPBELL

My mother loved to have a good time. She loved corny old jokes. She loved to bake peanut butter cookies, pressing a chocolate kiss into each one for a special little touch. And she loved to work with her hands—hour after hour, she sat at her sewing machine, deftly crafting Raggedy Ann and Andy dolls for the Silver Dollar City theme park in Branson, Missouri. She did beautiful needlework and often took her sewing box along when she went to livestock sales at the stockyards with my dad. While Dad bought and sold cattle, Mother sat beside him and lovingly embroidered pillowcases.

My kids remember all my mother's hobbies—and much more about their grandmother. They loved crawling into the pickup with Mother and heading to the field where Dad was working. Dad would turn off the tractor and join them for a tailgate picnic.

All of her older grandchildren have many happy memories of her, like the year they went home with their grandma during Christmas vacation. During their stay, a surprise snowstorm filled the roads with huge drifts. The kids were a bit concerned that they might not get home for Christmas, but they were nonetheless in no hurry to leave Grandma and Grandpa's.

My youngest daughter laughs now about the suitcase she once packed for an overnight visit. Otherwise empty, the suitcase rattled with a leftover paperclip and a rubber band. Why bother to take clothes when she knew Grandma would let her sleep in Grandpa's pajamas?

Another favorite memory that haunts my kids is of the baby pig that their grandma kept in the kitchen. The runt of the litter, the squalling little piglet was too weak to stay in the barn. So the pig lived in the kitchen, next to the stove, until it got strong enough to go back to its mama—just like in Charlotte's Web. The kids loved to sit and hold that little pig, and they never minded that they smelled like a pig after they played with it. (It doesn't matter whether a piglet lives in a kitchen or a barnyard; it still smells like a pig.)

But the younger grandchildren have none of those memories. They don't remember how their grandma grabbed the camera every time one of them did something cute. They don't remember her sitting and reading Bible stories to them before bedtime. They never saw the way this happy, life-loving woman laughed and played with her grandchildren.

Alzheimer's disease changed Mother from a cheerful grandma who loved to have a good time to a small, confused woman. By the time her youngest grandchildren came along, their grandma couldn't form words the way she used to—she couldn't tell jokes or laugh or read Bible stories. And she sometimes did things that didn't make sense, which frightened the smaller kids.

Mother cherished the children so much, and I desperately wanted them to remember her as someone fun and caring and beautiful. But what was there for them to remember? The youngest ones were only toddlers when Alzheimer's first entered our lives, and the disease had taken their vibrant grandmother away before they had a chance to build memories of her. How were they going to remember this special woman?

Lord, please help them remember their grandma's light heart and fun spirit, I prayed.

One night, she and I sat together on the couch. She held her precious box of embroidery thread and pillowcases on her lap. Oh, how she had loved to embroider.

She gingerly lifted the tin lid. Lovingly, she took out one of the delicate linen pillowcases. "Look at this," she said—or tried to say. Sometimes she got the right words out. Other times, the only sounds that came from her mouth were not words. Just gibberish.

I stroked the smooth, strong fabric, and then she carefully put them away. A few moments later, forgetting that we had just looked at the pillowcases, she opened the box back up. "Look at this," she said, and we looked at each one again.

That was one of the last times she looked at her pillowcases. Her mind no longer allowed her to do the embroidery work she loved.

A few years later, Mother died, and my dad gave me the box of pillowcases. I took them home and put them in an old trunk, not sure what to do with them.

They stayed in the trunk for several years. And then one day in early December, I was thinking about Mother and the grandkids, and suddenly I knew what to do. Those beautiful pillowcases were perfect for passing on memories of a grandmother's love for her grandchildren. I would make them into pillowcase dolls. If I hurried, I could get them done in time for Christmas.

I opened the old brown humpback trunk and pulled out the yellowing pillowcases. Many of them were beautiful, for Mother was a perfectionist. She had done lovely cutwork embroidery in a dainty satin stitch, and then cut out each tiny open space with her sharp embroidery scissors.

I washed the pillowcases, and then carefully began to cut and sew. Every pillowcase became a doll for my children, grandchildren, nieces, and nephews. And when the dolls were finished, I looped small notes around the dolls' necks explaining how much Grandma loved to sew and what great pleasure and pride she took in her work.

Mother would not have been pleased with some of the pillowcases, for those she embroidered in the last few years were far from the perfection she demanded of herself. As her mind deteriorated, she sometimes got the designs upside down and off center, and many of the stitches were long and shoddy. But when I turned them into full-skirted dresses on the dolls, the flaws were not evident. Only the beauty of the dolls showed, Mother's memory swaying with the soft fabric skirt.

When we lost Mother, we did not lose our good memories of her. Today, twenty-four dolls in dainty pillowcase dresses bring back memories of Mother's happy days—those days when she got out her skeins of brightly colored thread and worked on her pillowcases. She loved dolls, too, and I like to think she'd be thrilled to see my handiwork in her handiwork as the dolls sweetly sit in places of honor in their new homes.

Mother's grandchildren don't all have the memories, but she left them something of herself. Their pillowcase dolls tell the story of a special, loving grandmother who made beautiful things. ⬡

A righteous man will be remembered forever.

PSALM 112:6

Dear Heavenly Father,

Thank You for my mother, Lord. I know she wasn't perfect. But today I choose to open my eyes to the good gifts she gave me— for the way she supported me, for her love that seemed to have no limit. Thank You for teaching me so much through her, and thank You for the effect she's had on my life.

Lord, I pray that You would help me follow in my mom's footsteps—make me the mother You want me to be, Lord.

If I had my life to live over,
instead of wishing away nine
months of pregnancy, I'd have
cherished every moment of
my chance in life to assist God
in a miracle. I would have sat
on my lawn with my children
and not worried about the
grass stains. When the kids
kissed me impetuously, I would
never have said, "Later. Now
go get washed up for supper.

ERMA BOMBECK

Seize the Day

They get a little bigger every day. And each day goes by so fast—it's so easy to get bogged down in the whirlwind of rides and lunches and science fair projects and forget to relish each moment we have with our kids. But it's never too late to tickle and laugh and just enjoy being together. There's no better day to start than today.

But encourage one another daily,
as long as it is called Today.

HEBREWS 3:13

At the end of your life, you will never
regret not having passed one more test,
not winning one more verdict or not closing
one more deal. You will regret time not spent
with a husband, a friend, a child, or a parent.

BARBARA BUSH

Quality Time

LOUISE TUCKER JONES

When my oldest son, Aaron, was in high school, one of his favorite bands came to town, and he was so excited as he made plans to attend the show with our church youth group. I knew he'd have a blast with his friends, but to my amazement, he invited me to come along too. He knew I liked one of the opening acts, and I readily accepted his invitation.

But by the time the concert rolled around, I wondered if I should be going. My youngest son, who has Down syndrome and progressive heart disease, had been ill for a few weeks, and I knew I'd be worried about him all evening. My husband countered my doubts and encouraged me to go to the concert, assuring me he was quite capable of taking care of our youngest. I wavered.

Finally, reality hit me: Aaron was sixteen years old. How many opportunities would I have to do something fun with him before he went away to college? And how many teenagers actually invited their mothers along to a concert that was clearly geared toward people under the age of twenty? The decision was obvious. I couldn't pass up this opportunity.

When we got to the arena, I sat with Aaron and his girlfriend on the third row, surreptitiously stuffing cotton in my ears to block out the ear-splitting bass tones of the first act. For the rest of the night, I stood when the kids stood, clapped when they clapped, and tried not to let anyone know how nervous I was to feel the floor vibrate beneath my feet. Aaron and his friends were amused at my display of enthusiasm. And I had a great time.

By the time we stepped out into the startlingly quiet night air, I was certain my hearing was damaged forever. My ears were ringing, and the kids' voices and the squeak of the car door seemed muffled, but my deafness quickly passed. So did my son's teen years. In no time he was in college and away from home. I missed him in a way I couldn't have imagined. But on those days when I was especially lonely for his ready smile and his teasing manner, I would think back to that concert and be thankful once again that I didn't miss the chance to spend time with my son.

Aaron is now grown and we are still very close. Some days

he calls between classes at the university where he teaches just to chat and tell me about his day. I drop everything and enjoy the moment, knowing these times too shall pass.

We sometimes reminisce about that concert—sometime in the course of that evening, we made a memory that would last a lifetime. And to this day, Aaron still laughs that the only person in the youth group to get an autograph that night was his mom. ⬡

Whenever we have the opportunity,
we should do good to everyone,
especially to our Christian
brothers and sisters.
GALATIANS 6:10 NLT

The Picnic

NANCY B. GIBBS

Kim sat on the picnic table and watched her kids and husband as they played. The boys laughed as they skipped rocks on the pond with their father, and her daughter giggled as she fed bread crumbs to the ducks. Suddenly, Kim was overwhelmed with an awareness of how much God had blessed her family.

Her heart swelled with pride when her little girl ran over to give her a big hug. "Thank you for the picnic," Elizabeth shouted.

Kim understood again how important it was to spend quality time with her children. Even though her work schedule was demanding and it had been hard to find time for a family outing, she knew that the memory she made today would last a lifetime.

Work will always be around, she decided, but the children have a way of growing up way too quickly. ⬡

Outings are so much fun
when we can savor them
through the children's eyes.

LAWANA BLACKWELL

You have a lifetime to work,
but children are only young once.

POLISH PROVERB

All Too Quickly

STEPHANIE WELCHER THOMPSON

When our daughter, Micah, was two weeks old, I wanted to have her portrait made at a local studio. Flipping through the photographer's portfolio, I saw darling black and white shots of sleepy, naked, newborn babies.

"That's what I want," I said, pointing to a bald baby lying facedown with her legs curled underneath her stomach and her bottom in the air.

Another pose showed a nude baby held in his daddy's hands. Precious! Micah barely weighed five pounds, and I wanted naked photos to emphasize her skinny legs and tiny arms. I made an appointment for an evening later that week, thinking Micah might sleep during an evening appointment and I could get one of those dreamy, ethereal baby shots.

As we drove to the studio, Micah cried and yelled from her car seat. It was only the second time that she'd been in the car since she came home from the hospital. The wintry streets were dark as my husband drove us to the appointment. I didn't know then that

Micah was afraid of the dark.

Since birth, Micah seemed fussier in the late afternoon and
evening hours. She had the symptoms of colic, crying inconsolably.
What was I thinking, making a nighttime appointment?

"You know every time we take her clothes off, she screams,"
my husband reminded me as we pulled in front of the studio.

Inside the studio, Micah did not sleep.

"Take your time and nurse her," said the photographer. "That
will make her more cooperative."

Micah nursed a little, but mostly she just felt like screaming
and crying. She wanted no part of the naked photo shoot, even
when I wrapped her in a blanket. Later in the session as I held her
bare body in my hands, she pooped in my palm. The photographer promised she'd take a lot of shots to ensure a good variety,
but I doubted she'd get a good one.

Weeks later, I picked up the proofs and even though there
were no sleeping baby poses, there were quite a few cute pictures.
It was another three weeks before our prints arrived.

Yesterday, I took the photographs to be framed. Amazed, I
stared at the tiny little infant in the picture. Micah is now three
months old, seven pounds heavier, and five inches longer than the

newborn in those black and white portraits. I hardly could believe our baby was once that small. I'd forgotten how frail she was, how the skin on her arms and legs hung in wrinkles.

Micah's pictures awakened me to the realization that she is developing more than I notice on a daily basis. Days turn to weeks, time creeps by, and one day my baby will be grown. Instead of a serene, sleeping baby portrait, I got an important lesson in parenting: Time is short, and I need to relish each day with my baby. I need to cherish each phase of her life—and, of course, take lots of pictures along the way. ⬡

Teach us to number our days aright,
that we may gain a heart of wisdom.

PSALM 90:12

Live in the Moment

There will never be another day exactly like today. Spend a little portion of your day simply interacting with your kids. Find (or make) a little time away from work, soccer practice, or dance lessons. Play a board game. Bake cookies. Savor the moment of just being together. ⬡

Every material goal,
even it is met, will pass away.
But the heritage of children
is timeless. Our children
are our messages to the future.

ANNIE DILLARD

Dear Heavenly Father,

The days are rushing by—so much to do, so many places to be—and sometimes I feel like I've gone an entire day without really connecting with my kids. Lord, I pray that You would infuse our days with Your presence, that we would seek You in the midst of all our busyness.

Father, thank You for every day I have with my kids. Give me a new awareness, Lord, of the special gift You've given me.

Acknowledgments